Works Volume 3:

by

Nicholas Boyes

Nicholas Jay Boyes

www.ecologicalera.com

contactnicholas@ecologicalera.com

Wikipedia articles are covered under the
Creative Commons CC-BY-SA 3.0 license.
http://creativecommons.org/licenses/by-sa/3.0/

ISBN: 978-1-329-05150-8
© 2015 Nicholas Jay Boyes. All rights reserved

Table of Contents

Introduction 5

On Modern America and Its Material Conditions 9

On Rent and Surplus Value 13

On the Historical Conditions of the Joint Stock 15

On Freedom of Expression and Speech in Capitalist Society 19

On the Material Conditions of America 21

On the Historical Conditions of Christianity 25

On Electrical Production and Biomass Fuel 29

On Disarmament and the War in Syria 31

Response to Barak Obama's Speech on Syrian Civil War 33

National Debts and the Bond Market 35

On Default of the Bond Market 39

On the Debt Crisis 41

On the Debt Crisis 43

On Universal Suffrage in America 45

On Apartheid and the Passing of Nelson Mandela 49

President Obama Shakes Raul Castro's hand in Public 51

On Rent and Taxes 53

On Karl Marx Theories of Surplus Value Volume 4 Capital 57

Events in Ukraine 61

On Taxes and the Wages of Labour 63

Some Conclusions to be drawn from reading Marx's Theories of Surplus Value, in Particular Part 4 of Capital, the Second Manuscript of Theories 65

On Recent Events In Ukraine 69

On Events in Ukraine..71
On the Conditions of the Worker in America............................73
On Milwaukee's Recycling Programme.....................................77
Letter to Greek Socialist Party On Greek National Debts.................79
On Crimean Russia and Ecology..81
Conditions in Ukraine..83
Letter to Russian Communist Party on Ukraine.......................85
Letter to Russian Communist Party on Jews and Putin...........87
On the Civil War in Iraq...89
A Little Philosophy off the Front in Milwaukee.......................93
On the Civil War in Iraq...95
Letter to Russian Communist Party...99
On the Workers Movement by Nicholas Jay Boyes................101
On the Continuing War in Iraq..103
On the Scottish Referendum..107
On Current Historical Material Conditions and Political Organization...111
Letter to Greenpeace...115
On a Free Press...119

Introduction

This edition of Works, Volume 3, was written during a time I was reading the 4 Volumes of Capital by Karl Marx. The Theories of Surplus Value, in 3 Volumes, were completed towards the end of the articles.

I read the books, and although it took about a year and a half, it was very rewarding. I learned a great deal, especially from the Theories. I had already read the 4 Volumes, so I sort of knew what to expect. Nevertheless really understanding the work was something the recent reading brought me. Previously I did not understand parts, and with Marx you have to read the words again and again before you learn the economic theories.

So it was with the reading of Capital this Works was written.

I liked the edit of the Theories, although the footnotes are absent; and in the first Volume of Capital the footnotes are essential. Friedrich Engels edited the first 3 volumes, so it is a different read than the Theories of Surplus Value that were not edited by Engels.

Some of the material may be a little misunderstood by me, there are, for instance, times wages can rise without surplus value falling. But it is true the surplus value is from the fund allocated to wages, as it is calculated by variable capital expenditures. The growing of capital, when considered relative to the surplus value contained in the commodity, may increase as the size of the total capital grows. In this respect wages could rise, and surplus value would rise too. This is a case of the machinery becoming more advanced, scale of production increasing when constant capital rises and also the variable capital. But if you consider profit, if we call constant capital C, variable capital V, and the surplus value S, V/ S is the surplus value, C +V/S the profit. In this case the profit would rise in a windfall effect, but as the machinery advances technologically, it becomes easier to function; it requires less skilled labour. So even if wages rose it would be temporary, until enough skilled workers were shed from production to be a more profitable capital.

As far as the profit naturally falling Marx's theory of value holds firm; that as the size of the capital increases, profit , C+V/S, results in less surplus value as there is simply less surplus produced as there are less workers creating surplus value. The quantity of variable capital falls relative to constant, and eventually this must effect the profit.

Compound interest also reaches a barrier to its expansion, as the amount of financial capital is reliant on how much profit is made in production, and it cannot forever go on increasing. This sounds obvious but it is not, as there are still notions of saving a dollar 100 years and having a fortune. Not only do banks rarely last near that long, if everybody did this the result would be default by most major banks. It is simply not possible for interest compounding to be paid off at some point.

These are just a few of the main points Capital brings out. Marx understood what surplus value represented, something Adam Smith, although a good writer often failed to grasp. Adam Smith did recognize what profit represented, somewhat, although he never refers to it as surplus value, therefore never dividing it into a byproduct of variable capital, rather he includes the constant capital in with the variable and surplus value, leading to all sorts of confusion. Adam Smith cannot explain how profits can fall while investment rises, as he does not connect the amount of labour, variable capital, with the surplus value in it. The surplus value would fall from larger investments, more constant capital, as less living labour is expended to create the commodity. 12 men working half the day for a capitalist, giving half their day unpaid, compared to 2 men working giving a half day, has to result in less surplus value. And at some point it has to effect profits. Productive capital that remained competitive, with the average rate of profit, would rise, a windfall effect when the new machinery was purchased. But soon, when other capitalists acquired the new machinery, the amount of labour time in the commodity would force the price down, as it would be easier to produce industrially. Adam Smith did not grasp this, probably because he only saw profit, not simply surplus value.

Introduction

The confusion of profit with surplus value muddles the water so to speak as it comes to appear the commodity produced as a material thing, and its exchange value, are how the capitalist profits. What I am trying to say is capital appears as a material thing, a commodity, rather than living labour. The labour is in the commodity, but this is simply returned to the worker after the surplus value is taken from wages. The worker is advancing to the capitalist his labour, and the capitalist is taking the product, selling it, and returning part but not all the value to the labourer. When approached this way it is obvious capital is control over living labour power. It is the ability to command living labour, and it is maintained by the worker not freely selling his labour, rather he must sell it to the capitalist who only gives him a portion of his product back to him in the form of wages.

If a worker was freely selling his labour to begin with he would sell it at its value. The bigger capitalists sell the product of labour below its real value, to drive out other capitalists. Adam Smith saw this. Profit causes the surplus value to appear as a separate part of the value of the commodity, an added on value above the investment. The capitalist can afford to not sell the product at its value, instead lower than its value, the amount of labour in it, to gain more market share on the other competing capitalists.

Monopoly then creates conditions to completely dominate prices, and increase surplus value to the maximum. The smaller capitalists are squeezed out; by selling below the real value of the labour contained in the commodity. Once established the monopoly stays until new technology makes the old production technique inefficient. The latter occurs at times, but the large scale capitalist still owning the means of production can often leverage their way into the new technology, resulting in a lengthening of the life span of the monopoly conditions.

It must also be said rent makes the entire value of the agricultural product sold. Of course, David Ricardo, who thought the lowest price land determined the value of a product, did not see the merciless removal from the land of the small farmer by the industrial farmer of the 20th century, who could sell agricultural products from better land cheaper than the worse lands and still profit. The confusion again of profit with surplus value. Even Adam Smith saw this selling below value of larger capitalists; it is unclear how Ricardo could have missed this economic reality. Today's rent is Mortgages and taxes. Taxes are a form of differential rent, better land, higher taxes, more value given to the mortgage holder. The large landed families are going away, with their noble titles to land ownership, but rent remains a reality, and it is still a means of creating surplus value from agriculture.

On Modern America and Its Material Conditions

The completely 20th century irrationality of the pattern of society of modern America, in particular its war machine, is visible in the new Millennium.

The material conditions of society are the reasons for the level of social development of a culture. While America may not be the developing world, it is not metric. Its factories are still not metric, and its industry continues to be built in the English system of measurement. It is the last holdout against the metric system, behind most all countries in the world.

It should be no surprise this is the empire most against all forms of communism...

The military machine the Aircraft Carrier the bourgeoisie is most reliant on has a nuclear reactor powering it. It sounds real high tech, but in reality it is straight out of the 20th century, before ecology was very important to the American capitalists, and consequently its military.

All one would have to do to end a major city in a conflict would be drive the large Aircraft Carrier ship near port and sink it to irreparably end all fishing, any industrial activity in port, habitation anywhere within hundreds of kilometers of the sunken melted down reactor. Use of this weapon is as irrational as locating nuclear reactors in large cities. It's like saying "if you attack me I will kill myself and you with me. Suicide bomber mentality....

And yet we still see the men marching off into battle, mostly aboard this suicide machine.

You can't even sink it in the ocean because it melts down and causes cancer to all who inhabit the ocean, including our non human friends, who also have sovereign rights to exist unharassed by the human being.

A nuclear reactor in a large city says the same type of thing; if you bomb the city and accidentally hit the reactor the city becomes permanently uninhabitable, the ecology ruined, for thousands of years. It is more like a human shield than a military strategy...

These 20th century material conditions were primarily given rise to by the attachment of the Americans to the work of German scientists they recruited for Project Paperclip after the German Civil War, also called the Great Patriotic War by the Union of Soviet Socialist Republics. The German doctors, all of whom were the reactionary bourgeoisie, whose programmes against the Jewish most resembled the reasons why the Jews came to America in the millions on the 19th century, fleeing persecution from Tsarist Russia, and Eastern Europe. Real modern and innovative.

Once established they were supposedly there to tell the Americans how to build jet aircraft, a component of the suicide machine we referred to prior to this. They built the missiles that also threaten the workers movements in Europe, the nuclear missile.

The nuclear weapon damages ecology, causing extinction of whole species. Only a fool would use one in battle, it destroys the very thing worth fighting for, any material wealth in a city becomes radioactive, and has to be disposed of in a radioactive waste dump for thousands of years. This remains as a weapon of defense for America, and there it is again, our aircraft carrier is also armed with it.

If a place were a worthless desert it would not be worth fighting for. The ecology is connected to the agriculture of a people, the rains from the forest of trees adjacent to it responsible for its harvest. In regions downwind from the sea we also see rains sustaining agriculture, for example California. Ecology also forms in the regions, like the Redwood forests of Northern California, priceless examples of the most advanced forests, Massive Redwoods, Douglas Fir, and Canadian Hemlocks forming a very advanced ecology with sovereign rights that transcend modern human culture.

On Modern America and Its Material Conditions

The point is these weapons, the missiles, jets, and probably other secret components of the modern American War Machine, were designed by Nazi Germans. It should be no surprise that while America fought on the side of the socialists in the German Civil War, once American material conditions came to more resemble Germany in the 30's, for example adopting another Nazi invention, the Autobahn, or Super highway, America turned against communism and went so far as to attack the peasant revolt in Indochina in a war ultimately lost by the bourgeoisie.

The material conditions of a society determine its social and ecological development. America is in many ways still in the last millennium, its measurement system is just another example. Its material conditions taken from Germany's scientists who were a reactionary bourgeoisie, still affects the culture today.

Nicholas Jay Boyes
Milwaukee Wisconsin
American Democratic Republic
5 2 2013 6:46 P.M. Central Time (US)

On Rent and Surplus Value

The presence of the landlord, the personal embodiment of the capitalist and rent, can be oppressive to the worker. The rent arrangement makes doing repairs to the rented home nearly impossible.

The landlord is rarely absent in the life of the proletariat, rather he is constantly subject to reminders he does not control his environment, ad nasueum in an apartment building where he has no land, no garden, and no ability to tear out the walls and construct a better environment indoors for he and his children.

The revolutionary nature of home ownership cannot be stressed further. To be able to disconnect the rent arrangement, with the worker owning his own home, has to be considered a movement towards socialism.

Surplus value is the origin of the rent arrangement; the worker in production creates the wealth that is split off the surplus value of the capitalist, and directed to the landlord. The landlord is like the priest and financial capitalist, all take a part of the surplus value created in production.

In the current idea of profit. the money (surplus value) created by keeping the worker in wage labour, and the value of the means of production, raw materials, etc, are all totaled together in the idea of profit. The flaw in this is all wealth is created by living labour. The surplus value is the part of the workday that is unpaid to the worker, and in order to understand it properly Marx called it surplus value, and said it was part of variable capital, the money destined for paying wage labour, not constant capital, the value of the means of production.

It becomes important when we are looking at the process of production we understand where value is really created, and the surplus kept by the capitalist.

So rent is a division of surplus value. The capitalist splits it off then it gets in the workers hands; this is calculated for by the capitalist that this sum of money will be paid for by the worker, to the landlord.

This why home ownership is revolutionary: there is no landlord. The bank and the tax system are the only vestiges of rent left, and the prior can be paid off eventually.

The mortgage may remind one of the landlord, but the bank owns it, and is not an active presence in the home, like the ever present landlord. It is less oppressive than not being allowed to work the land, with the spade. The rent is the price of the land after the immediate value of the structures on it, calculated by the average rent in the area. Socialism would have to be everyone owning their home. It is the only logical alternative to a landlord. It is achievable as a goal of the revolution, and although a house may be considered an investment of sorts, it is still the abolition of a form of rent, and the end of the most obvious form, landlord.

Nicholas Jay Boyes
Milwaukee Wisconsin
American Democratic Republic
6 4 2013 8:39 P.M. Central Time (US)

On the Historical Conditions of the Joint Stock

The idea of partial nationalization of a joint stock company is condoning the creation of surplus value from its operations. Owning even a majority stake in the company by the state still allows for the creation of surplus value.

Why would a proletariat profit off his own labour? The surplus value advanced to the capitalist without the real consent of the worker.

The worker does not freely labour for the commodity he produces. He is not selling his labour by choice, he is spurred to work to survive, and if he is doing more than just surviving this is a cost of production to the owner of the company, often gained through unions and strikes. Wage labour presupposes the non ownership of the means of production by the labourer. Wages are determined by the minimum amount the labourer needs to survive, and keep laboring.
"Profit sharing" simply means if the capitalist makes profit the labourer gets to share in the wealth, in other words, costs for labour rise, otherwise known as an increase in the variable capital expenditure.

State ownership of a portion of a joint stock company is the labourer making a profit off himself. As all wealth comes from labour, this is obviously absurd...

Furthermore even if wages rise it is condoning the exploitation of wage labour, as bourgeois management is still the government of the economic structure of capitalism in the factory.

Lets face it, if the state got a commanding share of ownership of the joint stock company, say, 51% of the shares, and started trying to raise the cost of labour, profit sharing the wages, what investor would keep their money in a more expensive arrangement? They would bail out the first chance they got, and put their money where maximum gain was the goal.

Thus we see the fallacy of partial ownership of the means of production by wage labour when the company is still creating surplus value, management and supervisor the government of capitalists. Wage labour costs rise, and the surplus value, simply the value of the non paid section of the workday could be more difficult to maximize, resulting in capital moving investments elsewhere to more profitable companies.

The 8 hour day at a socially acceptable wage would be a more direct way of reducing the influence of the bourgeoisie. Profit sharing is nothing more than a small reduction in surplus value from a company, yet condoning the structure of production for a greater amount of relative surplus value. And the joint stock ownership of the company still makes profit, even if the workers get a small raise. Of course, even if the company is only nationalized for a short time, for example General Motors and Chrysler, obviously the unionized workers are removed at the most politically convenient time.

All profit stems from wage labour. As we have seen, a worker profiting off himself is absurd. Partial nationalization will never free the labourer from the bonds of capitalism, it will only raise wages in an environment of less skilled labour required to produce a commodity every time the means of production are further progressed, increasing pressure to move capital or remove better paid wage labour. Nationalization can still be effective when there is no money paid to the owner, simply a direct change to the workers who have been creating the wealth enjoyed by the capitalist, if it was workers under a revolutionary state, where speculation on states debts, bonds, for example, which are indirectly a means of profiting off the partially nationalized company, are replaced by a workers government. The idea is to keep the means of production from exiting due to the desire of the capitalist to simply move the factory when a government is elected socialist and watch economic conditions decline, unemployment rises, more paupers, a greater unemployed reserve army of the proletariat...

Russia has been promoting this example of capitalism, partial nationalization in a joint stock company. Workers should realize

On the Historical Conditions of the Joint Stock

Russia no longer is a revolution. Partial nationalization is an increase in variable capital costs, to be removed as soon as possible by management. No capitalist in his right mind would place his money in a less rather than more profitable company, which is exactly what raising the wages under partial nationalization does.

Nicholas Jay Boyes
Milwaukee Wisconsin
American Democratic Republic
6 28 2013 11:28 P.M. Central Time (US)

On Freedom of Expression and Speech in Capitalist Society

The current position regarding the works of political economy and philosophy of Karl Marx is one of confusion. After reading many of Marx's writings, and publishing books about Karl Marx, in particular my work on the Economic and Philosophic Manuscripts of 1844, the Introduction to Critique of Political Economy (Grundrisse) and the first manuscript of the German Ideology, all published recently and available through Lulu, my publisher, I have come to a realization: Karl Marx wrote about philosophy and political economy. I know this sounds obvious, but there are some who would have us believe Marx wrote on military topics.

The closest I have seen Marx write on military topics I have written about in Works Volume 2, on the American Civil War. Marx sided with the North, against the secessionist slave owners, and supported Abraham Lincoln. What he did not do though, was give directions on military strategy.

He also attempted to travel to the Paris Commune, and was detained by French Police. He felt the Commune was a good effort, but again, did not order the Communards in battle.

This leads to a popular misconception that Marx's work was all directed at violently overthrowing capitalist society, that Marx and his work was a violent effort at dividing the democratic governments of Western Europe in particular.

In my studies I have found: I cannot say Marx was a non violent Mahatma Gandhi figure, but Marx is not writing about how to have Civil War, as in tactics of violence, troop movements, etc.
Marx was attempting to understand the historical material progression of capitalism to socialism, and the breakdown of the Guild system and Feudalism in particular. He came in a violent time, as is today all societies of the time knew war. In this respect it is strange he does not digress more about his feelings about war to overthrow the bourgeoisie. But this may come as a surprise to those unfamiliar with

Marx I am hard pressed to find any calls to war to help the workers, although war is the way most changes in economic structure in society seem to be settled now and today.

Instead all I seem to find is attempts to understand Adam Smith, Ricardo, Say etc.

Why is Marx so hated there is not a complete collection of his work in Chicago or Milwaukee's libraries?

I'm not expecting it to be taught at capitalist universities, but it appears to be censored. Why is this? Real political economy, a true scientific study of capitalist economics and philosophy being actively repressed and kept from workers view, by countries that claim to be in favor of freedom of speech and expression?

It is a sorry tale of deception, and fear of the worker that results in this censorship. To read Marx is to study political economy, not military warfare. This escapes our bourgeois thinkers of today. It is probably no accident as Marx and his Theories of Surplus Value and Capital remain the forefront of economics today, it is only the fear of the power of truth that drives the censorship. His theories ring true for much of his writings, and seem to be a complete set of works that can explain the true functioning of the capitalist economic system.
The material is worth reading. It should not be censored.

Nicholas Jay Boyes
Milwaukee Wisconsin
American Democratic Republic
7 13 2013 3:49 P.M. Central Time

On the Material Conditions of America

The real connection of the current political structure of America is one of a society formed primarily by Europeans, for example the Spanish, French, and the British. The British were always very tied to what was once their colony, which broke off in 1776, with the help of the French, who barricaded the British seaports from sending out the warships to fight the colonists who wanted to secede. The French settled in many regions of America and Canada, and the language is still the spoken tongue of Quebec Canada, although the Canadians have yet to break British rule. The Spanish settled in Florida, and were also involved with the Mexican settlements of what is now California and Texas.

The point is the traditional European cultures had a large role in founding the America and Canada.

When we think of these societies, such as Spain, we see today royalty still exists. In Britain too the royal family still plays a role, and the song "God Save the Queen" is still the British anthem. In Canada "Oh Canada" is now sung instead of the "God Save the Queen" British anthem, although it is not clear if Canada really follows the mostly ceremonial role of the monarchy.

And lest we forget Germany, who also settled in Milwaukee, Wisconsin in large numbers, many of who were under the Kaiser or Prussia. They also had a royalist history, and the powerful families of early capitalism there still exist in Germany and America today.

In all these cultures capitalism and its supporters, the church, the landlord, the taxman, were present in America. Although there is still a royalist presence in Europe, capitalism is currently ruling.
The parallels persist though, in respect to Jesus and the Jew. Christianity is in full force in capitalist Europe, in Germany Angela Merkle's Christian Democrats are in power, and even in France, where the Socialist Party is in power we see Catholics dominating the society, for example when America had an escapee such as the Edward Snowden affair, Francois Hollande closed the airspace over France to

Bolivia's leader Evo Morales, who was coming from Russia where the defector escaped to. The plane was not carrying Snowden, and all they did was show that France and the Democratic Socialists are not in favor of the proletariat. It would seem all merely political changes to Western society, elections that do not have a real effect on the economic system, show the futility of changing the economic system through the political.

Clearly capitalism is ruling, the economic system in charge of the political, in Western Europe as well as America, the two regions where the strongest capitalism has been practiced. All systems of society are subordinate to the capitalist economic system, the church, landlord, and taxman. And all are paid for by the bourgeoisie, with the profit gained though exploitation of the labourer.

In the uprising in the middle 20th century, the issue of nationalization was in the front of the conflict. Russia had somehow freed the worker from the exploitation of the capitalist, and had a revolutionary government. Western Europe felt threatened; the traditions of Christianity were going away, and the races of the people such as Jewish were mixing with their so called betters.

Eventually push came to shove and the resulting conflict resulted in most of Europe changing the economic system to one without private property, and the production for surplus value was removed. Half of Germany fell to the proletariat, although this was eventually undone later in the century. Nevertheless in the early 21st century it is still remembered with horror in the bourgeois press, and government of the Germans in particular, as well as most of bourgeois Europe.

As far as the East of Europe there is no longer any royalty to speak of, all removed in the 20th century by the revolution.

There are many who fail to see the connection between traditional European thought and material culture and how it affected America. The lack of the metric system is the main fetter on America's industry today, and where is the measurement system in use from? It is called the English system because that is how people there always measured

On the Material Conditions of America

in the last millennium. Direct import from our past, a traditional European material connection to our feudal past.

Those who fail to see the material causes of the economic nature of a society do not grasp materialism. The level of advancement of a people is reflected in their natural sciences, the daily life of the worker in industry rather than as a farmer, for example, are a measure of how anthropocentric and traditional a culture is. And capitalism has become today's traditional culture; you are born in to it, and labour is not the product of independent workers freely selling their labour. Labour in capitalism is forced, the Homeless Shelter the cure for labourers who don't fit in.

How could someone could look at Franco's fascist Spain, Catholic and the epitome of traditional, get the idea something radical was occurring? It's like looking at Hitler's Final Solution and thinking killing the Jews wasn't Christian. Why would someone so easily be taken? Hitler was a Christian, and his main General in the war was even named General Christian.

These traditional European cultures, like Spain who still has Juan Carlos as king, after 30 years of fascism, still influence America today. Their ideas are the ideas of a past era, when men killed the Native Americans in the Inquisition, and enslaved the African black man. The ideas were from Europe, and the uprising in the middle 20th century in many ways a kick from the traditional society that, yes, we still exist and are capable of reminding you in the most oppressive of ways, such as the Blitzkrieg.

They are gaining force through the lack of understanding by the workers of their common plight. The Allied movement created the United Nations to fight Nazis. It remains a pillar of the gains of the revolution, part of the Post War Dream of the earlier generations. Short of another violent episode like the last major war in Europe, the United Nations remains a check on this traditional European and American activity. The United Nations is not a perfect world, a paradise for the labourer. But the General Assembly represents most all of the worlds countries, and still exists today. It is not the North

Atlantic Treaty Organization, but is still victim to domination from Western Powers. And as capitalism reaches all countries in the world today, it may prove difficult to remove the traditional capitalist practices. Nevertheless a friendly relationship between the proletariat who founded the United Nations to fight the reactionary bourgeoisie in 1947 may still exist. It could be worth paying more attention to this groups activities.

Nicholas Jay Boyes
Milwaukee Wisconsin
American Democratic Republic
7 27 2013

On the Historical Conditions of Christianity

The early Christians, for example Cyril of Jerusalem (c. 315–386), Augustine of Hippo (354–430) were among the first to call themselves Catholic.

"The state church of the Roman Empire was established on 27 February 380 with the Edict of Thessalonica, when Emperor Theodosius I made Nicene Christianity the Empire's sole authorized religion. Unlike Constantine I, who with the Edict of Milan of 313 had established tolerance for Christianity without placing it above other religions and whose involvement in matters of the Christian faith extended to convoking councils of bishops who were to determine doctrine and to presiding at their meetings, but not to determining doctrine himself, Theodosius established a single Christian doctrine, which he specified as that professed by Pope Damasus I and Pope Peter II of Alexandria, as the state's official religion.

Wikipedia see:
State Church of the Roman Empire

Catholicism refers to the Western Catholic Romans, and Eastern Orthodox who also share this title with their western counterparts. In 330, Emperor Constantine established the city of Constantinople as the new capital of the Roman Empire, where Byzantium and Chalcedon, settlements of the Athenian Greeks in ancient times, had stood. Constantinople was named after Constantine, first Emperor of the Romans who was a convert to Christianity.

Constantinople would stay as a single ruling unit in the East after the sack of Rome by the German Odoacer, an illiterate warrior who became the new King of the Romans after the sack in 476. This in many ways marks the start of the Dark Ages in Western Europe. It was the end of the Roman Empire, and much industry, or at least what little there was in the west, began to cease to function. Christian Princes became the dominating feature for about a millennium. The great distances involved in travel was the start of the tariff, a tax paid to guards during transport in Europe of needed products. Europe was reduced to a far more agrarian state in these years...

Constantinople would stand as the center of Eastern Christianity until the Crusades sack of the city in 1204.

"On a popular level, the preaching of the First Crusade unleashed a wave of impassioned, personally felt pious Christian fury that was expressed in the massacres of Jews that accompanied and preceded the movement of the crusaders through Europe, as well as the violent treatment of the "schismatic" Orthodox Christians of the east.
Wikipedia
Crusades

The Crusades would continue for hundreds of years, eventually by some strange logic and unbelievable events, the Eastern Orthodox center of Constantinople would be sacked by the Western Catholics.

"The crusaders inflicted a savage sacking on Constantinople for three days, during which many ancient Greco-Roman and medieval Byzantine works of art were either stolen or destroyed. The magnificent Library of Constantinople was destroyed. Despite their oaths and the threat of excommunication, the crusaders ruthlessly and systematically violated the city's churches and monasteries, destroying, defiling, or stealing all they could lay hands on; nothing was spared. It was said that the total amount looted from Constantinople was about 900,000 silver marks. The Venetians received 150,000 silver marks that was their due, while the crusaders received 50,000 silver marks. A further 100,000 silver marks were divided evenly up between the Crusaders and Venetians. The remaining 500,000 silver marks were secretly kept back by many Crusader knights.

Wikipedia
Fourth Crusade

What would follow was the Catholic takeover of the lands once belonging to the Eastern Catholics, the Eastern Orthodox, and the loot from the city being greeted with open arms by Pope Innocent, all gained through the sack of Constantinople.

As this was occurring the Catholics were also fighting the Muslims. They too were a target of hatred by the Knights Templar, and there were Crusades to remove the Muslims from Jerusalem although they never quite took control of Israel.

On the Historical Conditions of Christianity

The Knights Templar conquered what was Old Prussia in the 13th century. The name Prussia derives from the previous title. In 1308 the Teutonic Knights conquered Poland and began their expansion westward. And with them came their anti Semitism...

"Prussia entered the ranks of the great powers shortly after becoming a kingdom, and exercised most influence in the 18th and 19th centuries. During the 18th century it had a major say in many international affairs under the reign of Frederick the Great. During the 19th century, Chancellor Otto von Bismarck united the German principalities into a "Lesser Germany" which excluded the Austrian Empire.

Wikipedia
Prussia

Karl Marx would be exiled to France then England promoting free speech against the expanding Prussian forces. Many millions of Jews would flee the savage anti-Semitism in the Prussian regions for America, as well as much of Eastern Europe, in the 19th century. Later Adolf Hitler would annex Austria, although it was never really a part of Germany it was the Austro Hungarian Empire. Even the first World war it was not a part of Germany proper.

Christianity justified many events in the past that by modern standards would seem absurd. It was the cause of the anti Semitism of the Crusades, as well as throughout Eastern Europe into the present. The Old Testament is the worst of the anti Jewish writings, look at Ezekiel. The Christians seem to be ready to create the most fantastic stories, aliens, spaceships, extraterrestrial contact, if it includes conquering the Jewish.

In the movie Agora the real history of Alexandria and the Great Library is told. It is a forgotten history, much like most of the start of the Dark Ages, days of knights, and princes. In the film it is clear the Christians were a group of people who believed the world was flat, and consequently destroyed the Great Library of Alexandria, one of the 7 wonders of the ancient world. The scientific and philosophical writings of the ancients were burned, in the name of the new faith of the Roman Empire, Christianity.

As an import to America this religious group, although subordinate to the bourgeoisie as of late, has millions of adherents. The Church, an organ of the bourgeoisie, gets its money after the surplus value is created in production. The magnificence of the churches architecturally point to their high cost to build. Clearly they were not paid for by passing around a plate and the faithful simply leave a few bills. No, this religion requires large amounts of money for its leaders, who have figured out a way to get out of working, and their dwellings and places of organized worship.

The lack of formal separation of church and state in America is present as evidenced by the continued attempts to stop the elected school board governments from having any say over the method children are educated. The State pays for the Catholic school; it is called "school choice". The state under the bourgeoisie directly gives money to support the church, under the guise of "private schools". Clearly the church and state are not divided in America. The elected government loses control of the education of children, leading one to wonder how long this school board will continue to be elected, or simply exist. America certainly accepts imports from the east, and Christianity is a massive one. It is a historical phenomenon still present under the late stages of capitalism, and as long as the man making the profits continues to exploit the worker, it would seem here to stay....

Nicholas Jay Boyes
Milwaukee Wisconsin
American Democratic Republic
8 13 2013 7:57 P.M. Central Time (US)

On Electrical Production and Biomass Fuel

There are many ways to produce electricity. The whole idea is to simply turn a turbine, in most cases, (with the exception of solar panels). Hydroelectric dams also simply use the power of water to turn a turbine.

Nuclear reactors, coal fired electrical generation factories, gas energy generation , etc. all boil water to create pressure to turn a turbine.

Essentially all the turbine is is an electric motor run backwards, by steam pressure; you turn the drive shaft and the magnetic forces produce a current.

To boil water sounds simple, but in reality many methods in which great danger for the inhabitants, ecological and human, are used for boiling water. Nuclear energy is an example of getting carried away with what should be a simple process, boiling water, and making a mountain out of a molehill, so to speak. Generally when a country gets nuclear energy they get the 20th century weapon, the bomb. Nuclear waste also accumulates, and there is no real solution for its disposal. Coal is a logical way to produce electricity, when it is produced locally, like Chicago which has coal underneath it. The mineshafts are under the Chicago Museum, and Illinois has plenty of it.

Unfortunately coal is a fossil fuel, and causes acid rain. Acid rain gets into the Great Lakes and leaches mercury out of the stone when the PH level rises. This makes fishing dangerous, which could theoretically be a renewable resource. This is an industry in Milwaukee, there are Charter boats who take people out fishing, and they eat the fish. Hydroelectric is promising, but on the Great Lakes tributaries blocking the path of spawning fish and eutrophying the water is the result. Fish must be able to get up river to spawn, and less spawning means less fish.

Wind power is coming but like solar energy is still not cost effective. Nevertheless it is a very promising method of creating electricity in the long term.

Of course, to boil water sounds simple though. Biomass fuel made of Hay, harvested in the fields and pelletized could be burned. It is not a fossil fuel, and is in abundance. It is not turning corn, food, into ethanol, so does not have the stigma of burning food to a hungry person.

Pellets of biomass, simply compacted dry hay, could boil water when burned. Thus they could create enough energy to turn a turbine. Biomass fuel could be a way to cheaply and without much pollution create electricity, without nuclear waste, or fossil fuels. Hay is easy to grow in the fields, the farmers have balers. It just has to be dried and bales and a city could pelletize and burn this abundant supply of natural renewable energy.

Nicholas Jay Boyes
Milwaukee Wisconsin
American Democratic Republic
8 17 2013 10:41 P.M. Central Time (US)

On Disarmament and the War in Syria

America has made great strides in removing its Chemical Weapons, especially after the Cold War. They have removed, according to Wikipedia, as much as 90% of the stored up Chemical Weapons they had in the 80's. This is a sizable achievement given the vast size of Sarin, Mustard gas, etc., unpopular weapons, which was the main reason why this was done.

Unfortunately, in 25 years of efforts large quantities of Chemical Weapons remain in the arsenal of the United States.

The Chemical Corps have had the responsibility of removing these weapons of mass destruction. They number in the tens of thousands of men, whose purpose is to use Chemical Weapons and prepare for a Chemical attack against America, primarily abroad.

The recent use of Chemical Weapons in Syria, according to the bourgeoisie in America and France, by the government of Syria, on purpose, is another example of the need for an international treaty system to completely rid the civilized world of these weapons. But instead what do we see? Mr. John Kerry, a supporter of the American bourgeoisie, the Foreign Minister of Barak Obama's government, threatening to bomb Syria.

Why is this offensive? In the war Mr. Kerry fought in namely the Vietnam War, America used millions of Gallons of Chemical Weapons against the Vietnamese, to stop socialism. It was called Agent Orange, a Dioxin compound, to punish the workers who simply wanted a socialist society…

It truly is strange to hear this same voice, the voice of the public face of a man who is proud of his history as a military man in Vietnam, his main credentials as a politician, now against Chemical weapons in Syria.

How many more times are we going to see the pot calling the kettle black?

This continued contradictory activity; by a country that also has chemical weapons, and a large nuclear arsenal just in case they don't work, out disarming the world?

The only way to achieve non-proliferation is disarmament. If America is truly against Chemical Weapons, they should remove their own before rattling the saber at someone who might not have even intentionally used the offensive weapons. The United Nations has yet to reach a conclusion about the incident in Syria. In any case, it looks like do as I say, not as I do, like a priest who doesn't need material wealth, and gets to live vita communis, yet preaching the morality of capital to those whose due is to create material wealth, although not for themselves...

Nicholas Jay Boyes
Milwaukee Wisconsin
American Democratic Republic
9 3 2013 4:49 P.M. Central Time (US)

Response to Barak Obama's Speech on Syrian Civil War

The speech by Barack Obama, which I just watched on Television, was moving. Unfortunately, there were several omissions that should be noted.

To begin with, yes, Chemical Weapons were used in WW1 and WW2, both in battlefield conditions, although the latter was far better organized than the former. Of course, the next large use of Chemicals as weapons, from airplanes in quantities not of a single missile or explosion, as in Syria, was namely the United States of America in Vietnam. It was called "Agent Orange", and was a chemical weapon containing the most toxic chemical ever synthesized by man, measured in parts per billion, Dioxin.

The results of this are still present in the battle scarred rainforests it was sprayed on from air, millions of gallons to punish the Vietnamese Communist Party. Its legacy is a silent killer, creating many more birth defects and cancers than any missile ever used by Syria.

The next main use of chemical weapons was Iraq, although it was radioactive materials, with the same results of destruction we see in Syria. DU (Depleted Uranium) was used to cause radiation sickness in the Iraqis fighting against the American invasion. Its legacy is in Fallujah, for instance, where birth defects in children have drastically increased recently, making whole cities uninhabitable for thousands of years, the half life of Uranium, blown under the shifting sands by sandstorms, impossible to ever dig out.

Syria has agreed to remove the Chemical Weapons, but we don't yet know for certain as the United Nations has not concluded after several weeks what exactly occurred, regarding the Civil War use of Chemical Weapons.

America has yet to allow for the Russians to inspect American Chemical Weapons, or the United Nations. They still possess enough weapons to cause serious damage.

Syria is part of a biosphere in decay. Desertification has been growing steadily worse. The ecology is suffering, and needs repair, repair that will only come through peaceful labour at reforestation. Bombing Syria worse will not grow trees. Just because the ecology already messed up does not mean America should go in with boots in the water, a hundred Km or so off the border of Syria, where the territory of Syria may or may not be clear.

Syria did not get Chemical Weapons from Russia, yet Russia is still willing to take the toxic chemicals. How anyone could see Russia as stopping peace efforts is foolish. Obama could have said more about this new effort, which made much of his speech look outdated, like it was written sometime last week by the Pentagon.

In all fairness though, Obama did put off a Congress vote on Syria, and boots in the water, bombing Syria until the Russians make their move. That was good. But he is still involving the Army in a war overseas, just like every other president in recent history. And they do not always win. But the real loser every time is the ecology, from Iraqi DU to Vietnam Agent Orange. It has no voice but us, so rise up, and join reforestation efforts even if it is just in our own backyard.

Nicholas Jay Boyes
Milwaukee Wisconsin
American Democratic Republic
9 10 2013 9:00 P.M. Central Time (US)

National Debts and the Bond Market

The Bond market is the cause of the national debt. The national debt is a staggering sum in America, greater than the Gross Domestic Product for a year, that is, the total of all financial transactions of capitalism in a year, profit and all.

This money is entrusted to the state, and many believe erroneously it is used by the state for industrial projects.

This confusion arises from the fact if the state was to make surplus value off the project, money above and beyond what they paid out for labour the variable capital, and the constant capital, the raw materials and means of production, the money would have been invested at a profit, resulting in the interest being able to be paid on the debt by the state.

The fatal flaw in this argument is the constant push by capitalists to appropriate all worker owned property capable of creating surplus value. Any industry that can produce a profit for the bourgeoisie is immediately targeted for "privatization".

If the money in the hands of the state in the previous argument was being used for industry, as productive capital, this would never last long in the real world of capitalist industrial development.

The money put in the bond market is real money. It can be spent like any other. Consequently, it has to be put back if it is loaned, to the bond owner, with interest.

How can this money, which we now see is paid for by someone, a capitalist who is going to get interest on his investment, be used for state industry?

It is not. As we have stated above all productive assets of the state are always appropriated by capitalist production. The money is doing something else, and this is paid for as well.

How can this money create interest, surplus value for the capitalist, and why would it?

The capitalist state is controlled by the bourgeois, and the money is their bank account. It is money that could only make a profit if tied up by the state.

And how is it paid for? Another of the capitalists friends, like the church and the landlord, the taxman. The money is paid for by the productive labourer out the surplus value gained through production by the capitalist.

What this account really represents is not even means of production, or raw materials. This is a form of capital. It is control over the labour power of millions of wage labourers.

It is in this respect all arguments of the greater and greater sums of money, in bonds being supported by the state, is really a discussion about the control of labour power. The capitalist also makes a profit in production, on his factory ownership, he owns the means of production in a productive capital relationship, he pays the wage labour and keeps the rest of the surplus value, or profit. Beyond this we now have his friend the taxman creating some profits for him, as bonds.

It is really only a bit strange we even get to hear how big the national debt is. Capitalists generally keep how many hours above and beyond the wage labourers real need to work and keep himself able to work to themselves. Yet here it is; more than an entire year of stagnation of this market could occur without the capitalist making a profit, and he would break even.

Considered as financial capital the bond market is an attractive investment. It has a return in surplus value. But it is not investment in the state as a means of running profitable state industry. Rather it is a section of the surplus value divided off to the taxman, and increased by taxation. And as we have seen productive worker property is always expropriated by capitalists, meaning there is no return on the functions of the state.

National Debts and the Bond Market

Nicholas Jay Boyes
Milwaukee Wisconsin
American Democratic Republic
10 3 2013 10:33 Central Time (US)

On Default of the Bond Market

Today Barack Obama basically defaulted on the national debt. His statement to the press suggested without raising the amount of money coming into the state in the form of bonds, there would be no money in the state to maintain its functioning.

Currently there is an impasse between the more reactionary bourgeoisie, and more moderate members resulting in the state being partially shut down. Barack Obama now suggests he needs to spend the money being tied up for capitalists productively, the interest bearing bonds, on day to day functions of the state.

Thus we see the default already. Bonds are someone's capital. The state under capitalism does not produce commodities. Anytime the workers possess productive industry it is expropriated by capitalists to create surplus value, profit. We saw this with General Motors; the state finally getting hold of the company only to sell it off to the capitalists as soon as it was productively producing a surplus again. Where is the money to pay back the bond holder if it is not producing commodities? The state does not produce commodities under capitalism. Bonds are not borrowing money to productively employ it and make a profit, it is someone's money who intends to make a profit with financial capital. The state is subordinate to capital, the government is run by the bourgeoisie. It is not a bank. It is paid for with labour controlled by capitalists in the factory where the commodities are produced. Default is when you start to suggest you are no longer going to productively tie up the capital in the bond market and instead are going to spend it on your government.

The real question is who is invested in bonds who doesn't grasp this economic concept? Who would invest knowing there would be no return? One would think they would save their hides and massively sell off these bonds, as soon as possible...

Nicholas Jay Boyes
Milwaukee Wisconsin

American Democratic Republic
10 8 2013 2:45 P.M Central Time (US)

On the Debt Crisis

There is only one way out of the paying for the debt owed by the state Barack Obama suggested increasing of late, resulting in the partial government shutdown. As previously stated in my last 2 articles the state does not produce a surplus, anytime it does have productive assets they are expropriated by capitalists. Therefore state industry is not going to be able to pay back the interest on the national debt.
He must be honest about what a bond really represents, the discounted bill, something the proletariat pays for with taxes. He must raise taxes. If he does how long will it be before the whole system of the issuing of discounted bills for the debts of the state is exposed for what it is, that every discounted note (bond) from the treasury is really a raise in taxes.

Hard truth will then prevail. The bourgeoisie will have to reckon with their favorite trick, speculating on the debts of the state, exposed as a direct transfer of moneys to the state in the form of taxes to the coffers of the moneymen.

No longer will Obama's bailouts of failing non metric companies be paid back by anything but taxes, another form of surplus value. The fear of the state as a means of taxing the wealthy will be exposed as folly. The money of the state will be firmly bourgeois, taxes only another means of exploitation of the labourer.

Nicholas Jay Boyes
Milwaukee Wisconsin
American Democratic Republic
10 14 2013 9:13 P.M. Central Time (US)

On the Debt Crisis

With much debate there was a resolution to the problem of paying for the bonds by the capitalists yesterday in Washington. The solution seems to have been to indebt the state more, and speculate on the debts.

All American presidents do this. The only difference now is it is getting to be a very large amount of money, and the speculators were momentarily unsure of the government could foot the bill this time. Attached to the drama was a step towards national health care. It was designed to provide state money to workers who are in the unemployed reserve army of the proletariat, who have to work a few months then stop, as they are there for when the big orders come through for capitalists, then when completed, removed from their positions as labourers in industry. This group has a precarious existence, and of late their health care was not being properly provided for. We can only assume they must have been getting so unhealthy they could no longer work part time, they needed health care, so Obama provided.

The health care nationalization was what started the partial government shutdown, as the reactionary bourgeoisie was unwilling to pay for the health care nationalization.

The debate rapidly shifted to the debts of the state, as money was coming due. They waited until the last minute, and essentially raised taxes again to pay for the interest on the discounted bills from the Treasury...

The issuing of discounted notes, bonds, results in tax being paid to the capitalist who buys the bills. They are sold for say 93 cents on the dollar, and after 5 years they are paid a whole dollar by the Treasury. The discounted notes are used as an alternative to regular taxation, but really represent taxes being paid for every note that becomes due.
As we can see from what just transpired it is speculation on the states debts. Unlike money in a capitalist owned company, the money in the state is not currently present. This is the speculation, the money is not

going to buy means of production, or even to pay for productive labour; there is no capital present in the state. It is speculation on the ability for the government to repay the discounted notes, and the interest is paid for by taxes. Thus every discounted note represents taxes.

So essentially the way out of the crisis was as I wrote in an earlier article, the only alternative to default was to raise taxes. And that was precisely what Obama did with the debt.

As to why capitalist industry cannot productively tie up its capital without having to use the state to pay them interest on their money, the Great Recession still is present in American industry. The state offers a place with a favorable interest rate for capital, it is the national debt, all in bonds. It is real money invested, and represents capital, control over labour power. Imagine the millions of hours reserved profitably by the state in the trillions of dollars we see in discounted notes, and you see the real control of the economy by capitalists. It is staggering. And it was again increased at the expense of the worker who is forced to pay taxes....

Nicholas Jay Boyes
Milwaukee Wisconsin
American Democratic Republic
10 17 2013 1:40 P.M. Central Time (US)

On Universal Suffrage in America

The current pattern of politics in America remains one of a limited Universal Suffrage, a practice of the labourer being asked to support the liberal progressive bourgeoisie, or the reactionary bourgeoisie. It is a choice that requires workers to vote for the less oppressive alternative, which is obviously the Liberal one.

When a third party emerges, such as the one led by Ralph Nader, and takes enough votes away from the real power of the bourgeoisie, in this case George W. Bush and his Republicans, Universal Suffrage ends.

The interesting thing about the latter is the third party if anything was a main factor in the victory of Albert Gore, the progressive who won the popular vote yet was denied power by the reactionary Bush. The third party got more workers out to vote, and all this did was make a landslide of voters who preferred less extreme rule.

The memories of dictatorship do not heal quickly. America may have lost in Iraq, a Bush war, but they are still fighting in Afghanistan for a war created by George II.

Given the current political situation, it is looking increasingly like America will lose the war, as they have said already 2014 is the last year of an armed presence.

In Iraq they just left, like Vietnam. No parades, no real pride in having been in another American war overseas that pitted the workers of one country against the workers of another, for control of markets and capital.

What it really represents is a strategy of punishment. The reactionary bourgeoisie, now calling themselves the "Tea Party" are using the same strategies the Germans tried to use to stop the revolution in Germany in the 40's. The Eastern Europeans were upset at Jews and Communists, as they had always been resulting in the millions of Jews who migrated out of Eastern Europe to America in the late 19th century.

Out of the frying pan into the fire. America has never feared the Jew more than they do today, with the intense push to stop abortion, birth control, and the encouragement of police activities of spying on anyone who is not a Christian.

Why else would a Jew leave America for a worthless desert in Israel? The whole region it is so predictable. More equality always comes with more Islam. More Islam is no different than more Christianity, a society following a man who could not even read or write, Jesus Christ. He left no books, articles, etc.

By 350 B.C. in Greece Aristotle and Plato had written Philosophy books that are still relevant today.

The reactionaries punish the worker when they come to power. They arm the nation against socialism, and send out the workers to fight other workers overseas, even revolutionary ones like the Vietnamese, who fought to have more equality in their homeland. Even the oppressed races in America were made to fight; the black American risking and losing his life to keep apartheid type society in America in Vietnam.

So the choice is the reaction or the progressives. Voting is painless, and yes there is a choice. But the real power remains over the economic system, and even a black man of proletarian background, Barak Obama, if he wanted to as president of the republic, cannot stop the economic structure of capitalism.

The vote is a choice between the level of punishment the worker will receive. Given Obama's continuation of George II's wars, complete with the surveillance, there is not much choice, certainly not something to spend time promoting either of these representatives of the middle and upper classes, petitioning, demonstrating, calling people, etc. But voting for the less reactionary bourgeoisie is not hard, all you need is an identification card, and a short walk to the library.

On Universal Suffrage in America

The game is old. The French recently did it with Jean Marie Le Pen and Jacques Chirac. They ran the reactionary against the progressive Chirac, knowing people would have to vote for the les extreme candidate. Jacques Chirac won. But today we have the democratic socialists in power, so it could only slow down history so much. One would hope the situation in America could follow suit. Of course, the American labourer is the target of malice, and removal of the labour unions oppression. Better liberals than reactionaries, but it is not worth coming to blows for....

Nicholas Jay Boyes
Milwaukee Wisconsin
American Democratic Republic
12 2 2013 11:14 P.M. Central Time (US)

On Apartheid and the Passing of Nelson Mandela

http://en.wikipedia.org/wiki/Operation_Carlota#Operation_Carlota

This article in the Wikipedia, our most advanced encyclopedia, clearly shows how Cuba was a big part of the struggle against apartheid, in the Southern African region and South Africa, the country.

It is strange how little Americans know about this struggle. We were not taught this at the University, and the media has yet to acknowledge Cuba in the recent passing of Nelson Mandela, South Africa's post apartheid leader.

The really interesting part is how the Cuban Communist Party took the initiative. They first went to Southern Africa with 3 aging British propeller airplanes. They found success so got some boats together, and later the Soviet Union ran regular air service between Angola and Cuba.

The Cubans were a large part of African Independence movements in the late 20th century. Cuba acted on their own, it was later when the Soviet Union tried to take the lead, and they had failure. Cuba knew the territory better; they were there for 10 years since 1975. The second effort by Cuba was successful, resulting in solid defeats for the South African Army, which was the main protagonist, supporters of the UNITA bourgeoisie in Angola, where most of the fighting occurred in the anti apartheid struggle.

It truly is interesting to see all the American and Western European leaders with Mandela, considering Ronald Reagan made removal of Cuba from Angola a cause he armed South Africa to fight. His Vice President, George H. W. Bush (1) was the head of the CIA at the time of the fighting! They totally supported the apartheid movement with guns, missiles, mining equipment, etc.

Even George II had to express his sadness Mandela passed away. I wonder what his father George would have said if he would have known the way history would receive his (George I's) struggle...

Revolution can happen with a few men. It is a matter of rising to the occasion, and taking risks, even your own life. Putting yourself in the way of the logging truck in the Rainforest is the current expression of our civil struggle in America.

Cuba remains a revolution, ruled by the workers. The Embargo of President John F. Kennedy has lasted more than 50 years. How many more years will America punish the anti apartheid leadership of the Castro's?

Barack Obama recently stated his first political activity was against the apartheid system. The really strange part is he knows what apartheid is as he is president, yet imprisons and oppresses the Cuban people, by running Guantanamo Bay in Cuba, a concentration camp; and keeping the last 4 Cubans who visited the Miami Public Library on their visit to America and found the names of some of the terrorists, for example Luis Posada Carrilles, who were allowed to live in America. Just how much longer will this embarrassment continue?

Nicholas Jay Boyes
Milwaukee Wisconsin
American Democratic Republic
12 8 2013 11:36 P.M. Central Time (US)

President Obama Shakes Raul Castro's hand in Public

In a rare show of respect, at the funeral gathering for Nelson Mandela, President Barack Obama singled out Raul Castro, walked up to him in the midst of a number of leaders, and approaching Raul Castro, shook his hand.

This gesture, not shaking hands with anyone else, not being approached or forced in any way, and shaking hands with the revolutionary leader, was a welcome sign.

The only American president who ever shook hands with Raul's brother Fidel Castro was Bill Clinton. Instead he was constantly demonized by the bourgeois press, and almost never spoken to or shook hands with by American Presidents.

American apartheid towards blacks was real when Castro first took power. There were the familiar apartheid type signs on the door of the bar that told the African American female she was unwelcome among Europeans. It lasted until the Civil Rights Act of 1964, 5 years after the revolution in Cuba. Needless to say the Communist Party does not and did not practice what today we can only call racism...

South Africa seems to have created unity, albeit for a moment, in relations between America and Cuba. This type of acknowledgement of the successes of Cuba in the Independence movements of Southern Africa is welcome.

Raul looked shocked. He shook his hand, smiled, and put his hand to his heart in a sort of disbelief.

It truly was a good day. Hopefully Barack Obama will ease off Cuba to be capitalist, and lower that bloody embargo.

Nicholas Jay Boyes
American Democratic Republic
12 10 2013 7:25 P.M. Central Time (US)

On Rent and Taxes

"It goes without saying that when dealing with the composition of the agricultural capital the value of the price of the land… is nothing but the capitalist rent."

Karl Marx Theories of Surplus Value book 2 p. 307 (fifth volume of Capital)

After studying rent for months I finally found this in the end of the chapter on Differential Rent and Comment.

For some time I viewed rent and landed property as aristocracy, the old castles, estates of France or England. Here we come forward with something entirely new.

Marx always placed the taxman as the representative of the capitalist, like the priest or the landlord. It only naturally follows the taxman would be another recipient of surplus value gained from agriculture. The absolute rent of land is based on the lowest priced workable land. It is a form of surplus value, and is much like profit.

If the product is sold at cost price no rent exists. The costs of production can include taxes, though, and this is the modern form of rent. After deducting the absolute rent, the lowest tax, there is no surplus.

Differential rent exists when the taxman raises the taxes on the more fertile lands, and differs from absolute rent. Differential rent is the taxes on some agricultural land, of the same quantity of size but some more fertile than others being charged more for taxes for a farm producing more produce.

Differential rent is essentially property taxes for a farm, although the commodity is produced yearly. Our property taxes on our houses charge more to the taxman for better land and homes, and improvements in the land.

The absolute rent is the fact there is no free land in America. Although in America there was a time one could obtain land in the west for little or no cost, taxes and capitalist agriculture followed. Incidentally it was ecologically destructive to farm some land. It was even land that seemed good quality, but turned into the Dust Bowl, in years of the Great Depression of America in the 1930's. The taxes are not based on this though, any land in America is bought and sold, regardless of if it is so sandy it is only good for building a suburban type prefab home in regions of the south like the Carolinas…

In the Theories of Surplus Value applying the theories of Marx about rent to modern America is the important part. I could digress further on rent and will but I am still trying to learn it. It rests on the failures of David Ricardo, and on the real foundation of Adam Smith, the latter for his time a more realistic picture of modern capitalism. Adam Smith, for his failings such as his inability to grasp the real connection between surplus value and profit, instead only recognizing profit, wages, and rent (sometimes the constant capital, raw materials, etc. although more often than not ignoring this) as the creators of value, was a step forward from the Physiocrats, who only saw agricultural labour as creating value. But this is what Smith had to base his theories on. In this respect he is remarkable. Nevertheless the inability to separate surplus value from profit creates internal difficulties in his formulation of his theories of value. And Ricardo couldn't correct it.

In America all land is bought and sold except for state lands, where agriculture is not practiced. This is not to say state land is not productive though. We now know forests create rain, and the crops are stronger with trees planted near and on the farm. Logging is being replaced by recycling for paper production, it costs less to produce paper and affects farming as there are more rains and stronger, healthier crops. It is also campgrounds, which are an essential component of ecological experience. So even state lands have a value although they are not farmed, but the sale of this land is generally not practiced, it is for ecological and agricultural purposes and unfarmable.

On Rent and Taxes

Nicholas Jay Boyes
Milwaukee Wisconsin
American Democratic Republic
12 18 2013 11:22 P.M. Central Time (US)

On Karl Marx Theories of Surplus Value Volume 4 Capital

To begin with, rent is pure surplus value gained through unpaid labour. The price of land is the same as rent, for instance if a piece of land can yield a corn crop, it is sold not at the corn crops value for a year or two, rather for a longer time, based on what the land is capable of producing, its position near the city, etc. . Beyond the landlord we get to the taxman, who also obtains surplus value from the farmer, in the form of a differential rent. More on this later.

The presence of cost price, the difference between value of a product and its market price, assumes the presence of unpaid labour. The labourer is paid in wages, and the profit and rent are surplus value. The rent is the way the real value of the product is paid for. The rent is part of the value of the product, when there is no rent the capitalist can sell below value, because of competition, resulting in a market price that is closer to his cost price, which is constant capital, variable capital, and surplus value. Profit adds the value of the constant capital to the surplus value, the latter (surplus value) calculated by variable capital. The cost of the product for the capitalist is his cost of production, with the surplus labour his, so if he does not realize the full value and instead sells low, the value of the product is not realized. Rent takes care of the rest of this surplus, in the form of differential and absolute rent. Otherwise the capitalist can still profit, he just sells below the value of the product resulting in a lower profit, but a profit nonetheless...

The Phyisiocrats thought only agricultural labour produced a surplus. This was due to the industrial work in the cities being viewed as using the raw materials from agriculture, but agriculture was the cause of all industrial activity. This pattern of thought heavily influenced Adam Smith and David Ricardo, and Adam Smith sometimes reverts to it in the Wealth of Nations. Nevertheless his ideas of rent were very influential, rent on land in particular. Industrial capital can have rent, but rent on land and landed property was far more common in Adam's time. This confusion over unpaid labour; rent, taxes, etc. plague Adam's work, as he attempts to reduce all productive labour to wages, profit, (with constant capital most of the time), and sometimes rent.

Adam Smith did not see rent on land is the natural price of the commodity. The surplus is realized in rent, with profit and wages also realized. Adam Smith said rent comes only after the profit is made and, and wages were an essential part. This is the U turn Smith made, as he first says in Wealth of Nations rent, wages, and profit were the sources of the value of the commodity. He later says rent comes after the wages and profit are made. The cost price of products Adam Smith said was wages, rent and profit. Then he turns around and tells us rent comes after wages and profit are realized. This contradiction is present in the later chapters of the Wealth of Nations. First rent, wages, and profit (constant capital included), then rent as a subordinate form of surplus value. The constant capital was included in some of Adam Smith's work, but the surplus value is already on the raw materials from production, therefore the variable part of the capital is what produces the surplus value.

The constant capital, variable capital, and the surplus value are what the value of the product consists of. Rent on land is part of the surplus value, and surplus value is calculated by the amount of variable capital in the commodity.

Profit is calculated by the capitalist as including the constant capital, the total cost of production. This total cost approach can result in a lower profit and higher surplus, especially when labour is reduced as a result of the addition of new machinery, resulting in a ratio of less surplus value to variable and constant capital, but higher amounts of profit, for instance when the capital increases in size, and the volume of profit absolutely increases.

Profit can be less than the surplus value, when rent is present. The rent on the product is a portion of the surplus value accruing to the landlord. Taxes step in when the landlord is falling. Taxes are another form of surplus value, and the taxman is controlled by the bourgeoisie. The Treasury and the National Debt are not the property of the labourers. Rather it is a place to tie up capital not currently able to be productively employed by capitalists, with interest. It is capital, plain and simple.

On Karl Marx Theories of Surplus Value Volume 4 Capital

Nicholas Jay Boyes
Milwaukee Wisconsin
American Democratic Republic
1 12 2014 10:04 P.M. Central Time (US)

Events in Ukraine

The disturbances in Ukraine by the bourgeoisie, an attempt at Coup de Tet against an elected leader, continue. We saw one of their leaders from the United States address them recently, one Senator John McCain.

Clearly in statements like "we are all Ukrainians today" we see his hand in the violence now rocking the capital Kiev.

It would seem the more ignorant of the real meaning of what socialism is becomes, the more power and emboldened to violence become the reactionary bourgeoisie. The Nazis prey on the ignorant, like the church with missionaries. They are incredibly secretive, and mass in congregations of fellow want to be capitalists in ever increasing number. They war for control of markets, and direct their energies towards the coming revolution in which they will take their places as leadership and be allowed to run the economic system by expropriating workers property such as Cooperatives and nationalized industry.

Generally a racial element is present, the Jews and Israel a point of hatred by this overwhelmingly white Christian movement, and we remember Mussolini's hatred of the Slavic race.

The weapons of their warfare are sophisticated. Microchip implants, aircraft, nuclear powered ships. They are a product of the late stages of capitalism in the 20th century, totally reliant on fossil fuels and Uranium to power their machines of war.

Ukraine may fall, but not to the power of the argument. Communism and Karl Marx's theory of value remain leading ideas. David Ricardo and Adam Smith did not understand the mechanism of surplus value, they only understood profit and rent, and David Ricardo flip flops on rent, one minute it is subordinate to profits, the next an independent factor.

By placing the entire capital investment into a calculation of value, the profit and the cost price no longer reflects the true value of a commodity. The value of a commodity is how much labour is contained in it. Capital is control over labour power. Surplus value is calculated by the number of hours worked and number of men employed. Profit is surplus value divided by capital. Profit is not the same as surplus value, and profit can even rise while surplus value falls, or vice versa. And this is the main thing our friend Adam Smith did not grasp, and Ricardo only further muddled by starting out with profit and exchange value as measures of value.

If Ukraine falls to a coup de tet it is their own fault. Unfortunately it is the ecology and the children who are going to have to live in the society this creates. In time will this greed for gain prove productive? History may in time judge the real motives of returning to capitalism, and the conflict between capital and labour again rectified like we saw when Ukraine was socialist.

Nicholas Jay Boyes
Milwaukee Wisconsin
American Democratic Republic
1 21 2014 11:01 P.M. Central time (US)

On Taxes and the Wages of Labour

The system of the more capitalist parties in government constantly promising to lower taxes is suggesting wages will rise if they are allowed to more aggressively pursue what they believe being free to be, free trade, free markets, free enterprise, etc.

For the worker the promise of higher wages is compelling. Even if it was just a few hundred dollars a year its still a raise...

In reality though, tax, profits and rent are simply forms of the same thing; surplus value, the unpaid section of the workday. The profit would fall if taxes were lowered, when we take taxes as a form of profit.

This it is far more likely there will simply be a shift in the upper classes to simply increase pure profit, surplus value, by shifting around the money into capital.

So why even care if the money is simply being shifted around the pot of the bourgeoisie?

Wages are governed by the least possible amount that has to be paid for the labourer to continue laboring, if he is worked too hard or not paid enough he becomes too sick to work. That is the limit of the real wage of the worker. And it is the basis of capitalism, a part of the workday is unpaid, the value being appropriated by the bourgeoisie in the factory or on the land.

A capitalist has to train and insure for health a worker he brings in to the mill. It is far cheaper to simply work the labourer more hours, overtime, even if it is paid more (they still make a profit off the labour). Increasing profits create an incentive to work the worker harder, as it is cheaper than hiring and training a new worker.

The National Debt is capital. Paying it off is a bourgeois issue. It would be more in the interest of the worker if it were not paid off; it is command over the labour power of the human being, capital. The government's debts are not something the worker has any power over, unless we are to stop having capitalism.

So what exactly could lowering taxes do? If it was raising wages, why not simply state this fact? The tax taken from the check is a part of the profit, the latter being partially invisible. I mean to say it is not shared with the worker how much of his day he is not paid for his labour. All he sees are the taxes being removed, as it is printed on the check and he has to pay at the end of the year from what meager savings he has. Raising the minimum wage would be what these capitalists would have us believe they are doing. Less taxes, less profit.

All lowering of profit results in higher wages. It is a sort of strange dichotomy, every raise in wage or tax cut lowers the amount of unpaid labour the proletariat has to perform daily. More profit, more unpaid section of the workday going to the capitalist.

In this respect austerity is a rich mans game. It is toying with the worker, making him believe he is getting a raise. But the profit made in the unpaid section of the workday is not something he is privy to knowledge of. Therefore it is unlikely cutting taxes would raise wages, as it would just be treated like interest in the capitalists equations, never being paid to the labourer anyways.

Nicholas Jay Boyes
Milwaukee Wisconsin
American Democratic Republic
1 26 2014 4:09 P.M. Central Time

Some Conclusions to be drawn from reading Marx's Theories of Surplus Value, in Particular Part 4 of Capital, the Second Manuscript of Theories

The existence of rent on land is still present, in the price of the land, the mortgage on the land, and the taxation of the land. The price of the land has absolute rent, in the form of taxes, taxes that are present regardless of how bad the land is. The state is the capitalist in this movement, and as we have seen the state is run by the bourgeoisie, who use the moneys collected for bailouts, and support for their academics at Universities etc. who rationalize their economic theories. The state is not the property of the worker.

Along this same vein we come to the differential rent, the property taxes that tax according to the value of the land. It is not exactly clear how the farmers of today pay as much of the agriculture is so industrialized. The potato farm experience is unloading large trucks of the potatoes, sorting out good and bad on conveyor belts, massive tractors tilling the soil. In other words it is not farmer Hobart and a spade out back. In this respect it is not clear if agribusiness is even paying taxes.

Of course, a family farmer pays tax, differential rent on his property. He owns a dwelling and land, and this gets taxed. Competition forces him to be unable to pay the rent, large scale industry on the land, collectivization of agriculture, removes mercilessly the peasant farmer, forcing him into the city where he becomes a proletariat.

Purchasing land can be difficult. The bank often owns the land and the house on it, and 50 year mortgages are common. This is the rent, and even provides interest to the bank, who speculate on the prices of land and rent. The mortgage sort of resembles the serf master relationship, where after a certain number of years the Berger allows the serf working for him to buy his freedom from indentured labour.
Of course, even if the bank disappears and is paid off for the mortgage, the taxman remains.

Taxes are a form of surplus value. Unlike profit, or surplus value, the amount taken from wages is printed on the paycheck twice a month. Nevertheless this small window into the world of profit only creates an antagonistic relationship between the capitalist and the labourer. It leads to all sorts of ideas about openly profiting less, raising wages by cutting the taxes, which, as we have seen, would not increase wages, as wages are calculated by the lowest amount of wage required to continue laboring, nothing more nothing less.

In reality the bourgeoisie loves the state. It is where they park their capital, openly in the national debt, the financial power of this class owns more than the Gross Domestic Product for a good year in the bond market, the National Debt. It is capital, control ever labour power.

The surplus value created through unpaid labour is not shown to the worker. He does not receive a book at the end of each year explain how much profit was made in the year. He is simply not privy to the amount of hours he labours daily for no pay.

In this respect we see how the ignorant labourer could be convinced all he worked for that was objectionable was the taxes. They are a form of surplus value, and an obvious target. Of course, everyone knows ad nauseum through the television how the bourgeois live, in mansions where everything has a price. Basically a free for all where all is bought and sold, at sums astronomical compared to a wage labourers pay.

But the taxes pay the interest on the national debt. Even if it hardly produces interest, it is more profitable to buy bonds than stocks, or the money would not be parked there. In this respect it should be obvious the taxman is not about to give up his surplus value.

Karl Marx's Theories of Surplus Value is a good book. As it is the last 3 Volumes of Capital, is one wants to understand Marx I recommend it.

Some Conclusions to be drawn from reading Marx's Theories of Surplus Value, in Particular Part 4 of Capital, the Second Manuscript of Theories

Nicholas Jay Boyes
Milwaukee Wisconsin
American Democratic Republic
2 18 2014 9:52 P.M. Central Time (US)

On Recent Events In Ukraine

There was an event of interest in history today, a real Coup De Tet on Russia's doorstep. No pretenses of democracy here, the government of Ukraine was violently overthrown, by supporters of Yulia Tymoshenco.

It was remarkable in it was quick, had the support of the police at the end, and was widely supported by capitalists in the West of Europe and America.

In the old days overthrowing leaders sanctioned by Universal Suffrage like Victor Yanukovich was taboo. It was when Russia was convinced to have democracy the revolution ended. It was considered legitimate for Boris Yeltsin to bomb parliament (the Duma) as there were too many Communist Party members. It would seem the elected leaders were sanctioned by Universal Suffrage to any form of oppression of the proletariat, expropriation of workers property, closing the cooperatives, limits of freedom of assembly of the workers by ending unions etc.

Today we see the real face of capitalists, with the bloody struggle of body on body resulting in another nail in the coffin of the anthropocentric socialist experiments of the 20th century.
Victor Yanukovich was not the leader of the Communist Party of Ukraine. He wasn't even all that threatening to capitalists, tame compared to the old Soviet days.

Now we see Russia bordered again by the European Union, an alignment with the North Atlantic Treaty Alliance (NATO), who distinguished themselves by bombing socialist Yugoslavia under President Bill Clinton in America. It was dictatorship against democracy in the eyes of the world.

Perhaps they are getting desperate. Clearly Ukraine's Coup De Tet was never democratic, and was achieved through violence. There was never even any calls for new elections. Now we will have dictatorship in Ukraine, and no doubt if there is any Universal Suffrage it will be minus the Communist Party.

A historical day for the evolution of capitalism in Europe...

Nicholas Jay Boyes
Milwaukee Wisconsin
American Democratic Republic
2 22 2014 10:48 P.M. Central Time (US)

On Events in Ukraine

It truly is interesting to see Russia standing up for democracy in Ukraine. It is even more interesting to see America and Western Europe against it...

As a child we had to hide under our desks as the air raid sirens went off, because of the fear of socialism. We were told we were better than the Soviet Union; that because we had Universal Suffrage our leaders were picked by us and better than the Russians.

We were told the lack of democracy in Russia was grounds for building nuclear weapons.

Now we come full circle. Victor Yanukovych, the leader of Ukraine, sanctioned through Universal Suffrage, was overthrown in a Coup De Tet, last week. Within days Russia passed through the Duma the green light for war to Vladimir Putin. Crimea was the first region to be occupied, as it had a naval base in it leased by Russia.

The NATO was connected to the coup. John McCain firmly pledged his allegiance to the protestors who became the violent force that pulled the Coup. He went to Ukraine and spoke on stage to the demonstration of the more capitalist opponents of Yanukovych. He never made a statement against the violence....

In Yugoslavia Clinton told us it was dictatorship versus democracy. The socialists that time were killing Muslims. If only one could have seen what America just unleashed upon Iraq and Afghanistan. The latter NATO cooperated with!

Iraq too, same old message, better off without Saddam Hussein, as he was a dictator.

And now we see in Ukraine the elected leader of the majority of voters in Ukraine removed violently, and America and the Western Europe rattling the sabre at Russia, for standing up for democracy.

Strange. Furthermore Yanukovych was not even a socialist; he fought no battles for his people, and lived a sheltered life as a leader.
What if the Soviet Union had invaded West Germany and ruled as a dictatorship of the proletariat? Capitalists would have cried bloody murder.

Yet again we see the same old forces in society, capitalists, now removing democracy, and Russia, the opposite force not so long ago, ready to go to war for Yanukovych.

History provides no shortage of entertainment compared to fiction....

Nicholas Jay Boyes
Milwaukee Wisconsin
American Democratic Republic
3 2 2014 9:57 P.M. Central Time (US)

On the Conditions of the Worker in America

In my short adult life, at 42 years old, there are some things I have yet to see. One is the working class of one country ever fight for themselves, rather than being marched out to fight one anther on the front for the sake of markets by the bourgeoisie.

One could say I was lucky not to see The Soviet Union in the 70's. They may be right, but what I saw was the socialist movement peacefully fade in to the opposition, without nuclear war.

Iraq, Afghanistan, Panama etc. all examples of America going to war fighting the working class of one country against the working class of another, much like World War 1.

One example of socialism fighting betrays this; when the North Atlantic Treaty Organization (NATO) attacked Yugoslavia. America under the progressive liberal bourgeoisie of Bill Clinton aerial bombed what was a non aligned movement; not exactly communism, as all communist parties were supported or part of the Warsaw Pact of nations. Yugoslavia was not a Warsaw Pact nation, which tends to support they were close but not the real thing.

In some cases, especially Afghanistan, America fights peasant uprisings. Peasants and workers have one thing in common; neither own the means of production. They are forced to labour on land that is not their own, much like labouring in a factory not owned by the workers, rather than a cooperative.

If we look back at 95% of our living population who have fought war for the United States we see the current ruling power is very connected to Vietnam. In Vietnam, which was before my time, a more atrocious event occurred. A peasant rebellion was fought against by America, and the working class marched out to a war overseas to fight other workers and peasants who no longer wanted to have private property. This type of thing is rare today. As I said, at 42 I have yet to see this brutal shock of body on body between the bourgeoisie and the workers occur, except for Yugoslavia. Vietnam was not Yugoslavia; it was long, bloody, like Iraq and Afghanistan.

Korea was similar, when America fought the Communist Party shortly after the nuclear war in the region in Japan, where Hiroshima and Nagasaki were Atomic bombed. In Japan America fought alongside Russia, and the bombing by Harry Truman a cost of war for the Allied side, which included the Soviet Union, a group of labourers who at the time represented the International working class.

Unfortunately it is questionable what was actually accomplished; Japan still has an Emperor today, and Hirohito was the longest serving Emperor in history before his son succeeded him as of late.

Japan also remained and remains today a very capitalist country…

So Korea, Japans colony, in its chance at liberation from capitalism, fought America. China supported them. Again, this occurred well before my time. China had a revolution, and the Korea divided after the war into North and South. Another example of America's attachment to production for surplus value, a war that was fought against the very workers they supported in Europe at the time.
North Korea would remain divided over 50 years; both sides nuclear, South with many nuclear reactors, supported by the American Atomic Bomb as of late. North Korea would become a dynasty, ruled by Kim Jong-un, who succeeded Kim Jong –Il, his father, and his grandfather who fought the war, who started the tradition of the Kim family dynasty, Kim il-Sung. If they did achieve a socialist society it didn't last past the 90's as socialism is not a hereditary title to land ownership, or power. North Korea would go nuclear and test bombs, under the dynasty of the Kim's much later.

These examples still prove that in my lifetime I have yet to see anything resembling the American working class doing anything that looks like it would be in their interests; indeed, even in the examples I have given, except for the one I can't yet figure out, Yugoslavia. Before my time we have the obvious, Vietnam and Korea, there couldn't be anything further removed from proletarian equality in any on America's wars. Time to face up to fact; the American military no longer represents World War Two, which increasingly looks like nuclear ecological and social failure in Japan for America especially regarding the recent nuclear meltdown of Fukushima Diachi Reactor, built by General Electric. Is this our post war dream? There may be a few men in their 90's who remember when America was friends with Russia, but it is a fleeting moment. Rather we see another aggression on the horizon, Ukraine and NATO, both capitalist, and Russia, also now capitalist. Will we see the proletariat shed blood, workers blood, for all the protagonists who are countries with large Stock Exchanges and a class of capitalist owners in control of the means of production?

Nicholas Jay Boyes
Milwaukee Wisconsin
American Democratic Republic
3 12 2014 10:05 P.M. Central Time (US)

On Milwaukee's Recycling Programme

Milwaukee has been a leader in recycling for many years. It began at the Continental Can Company in the North side of the city. Continental was a production facility; they produced aluminum cans. As workers we were in the company, in a recycling center for aluminum in the front of the property in the 80's. We bought the cans back and paid the customers who we bought from.

Greenpeace reached us in the late 80's and I began promoting 100% recycling for Wisconsin. I was a Greenpeace activist. I posted recycling materials, wrote letters to government.

All the Union guys loved us. They would bring us their cans and we would pay them about $.40 a pound for them.

While we were still not metric we were handling tons and tons of scrap and cans. I used to run the baler, making briquettes and banding the huge stacks in the semi trailer.

Eventually our efforts worked, and although Continental would close, and eliminate us as workers in the early 90's, we achieved the start of nationalized recycling in Milwaukee, the Blue Can pickup outside all homes and apartments by 1995.

By the time the century turned we were recycling steel and aluminum cans, plastic HDPE 1 and PETE 2, paper, and cardboard in the Blue cans at the Street owned by the city.

By the next decade Milwaukee was recycling most all containers of plastic, all paper, as well as the steel and aluminum cans. Scrap production would continue to be a large industry in the Port, with a proletariat in production using cranes on rails, car crushers, shipping by Salties and freshwater Lakers.

It is 2014, and it is not time to stop. We must continue to stop the dumping of garbage in landfills. The next logical step is composting.

The divided garbage truck, capable of dumping two sides of a can into separate sides of the truck is all the way there. Simply put the compost in one side, garbage in the other. We could even use a light paper bag for convenience in the compost, it is biodegradable. All we now need to begin composting is an organized effort and some of those old oil containers in the Port of Milwaukee we could fill with compost and we're ready to go.

The compost could be used by the city, and the methane harvested for the motors. Compost is of great use, and other cites may follow the example, like recycling in Southern California, where good soil obviously could be a great asset to Los Angeles.

It should cost little and produce less waste for landfill, and could actually save money in the long run. Compost could even be sold, in its finished state.

Milwaukee is a leader in recycling efforts, and composting could be a logical next step in production.

Nicholas Jay Boyes
Milwaukee Wisconsin
American Democratic Republic
4 7 2014 10:56 P.M. Central Time (US)

Letter to Greek Socialist Party On Greek National Debts

Comrades

It truly is sad to see the continuing oppression of the Greek proletariat through expropriation of workers property. How long has this been going on for now? It seems all I read about is the continuing sell off of nationalized property, and no Co-operative development as an alternative to nationalized property, only expropriation by capitalists (of workers property).

The bond market is capital of the bourgeoisie. In America it is freely used as surplus value, and given to banks and other industries in bailouts for companies deemed "to big to fail". The amounts of capital are staggering, hundreds of billions of dollars. They only pay back their own fund, the national debt, so they can again use the state money to make profits.

In this respect I do not understand the debt problem Greece is facing. What I do understand is the debt is control over labour power, capital. Beyond this it appears just another mechanism to create a more capitalist society, and why it was not removed when the PASOK was in power indicates weakness, or a real lack of power of the political system to alter the economic.

In America the economic system of capitalism controls the political system. I can only imagine this must also be true in Greece.

I vote in elections but would never run in one, or take part in campaigning. It is nothing more that another form of a poll to me. I don't mind it, but it is not worth killing for....

So now we read

"State sell-off fund TAIPED is proposing the sale of a 67 percent stake in Thessaloniki Port Authority (OLTH), while it plans to revise the existing concession contract in a bid to make it more functional.

Ekathimerini 4 9 2014

Owning a percentage of a company is little comfort to a worker. It condones private property, and asks the worker to continue making profits for the capitalist. Wages are determined by the minimum of wages needed to care for a worker, so he can continue laboring for the capitalist. Even if he shared in profits he would still be a worker, and given capitalism functions on this latter principal alone no investor would allow this to stand for long. The higher wages would only upset the balance for the unproductive classes, middle classes, clergy, landlords, the taxman, in other words the bourgeoisie and its lackeys. The workers would be shortly forced to lower wages to make profits, as lower wages result in more surplus value, and vice versa, lower profits higher wages.

Greece has for to long been making these types of sacrifices for the so called betters of the workers. It is time to face up to reality that the national debt is just another form of capital, and just as we are not attempting to create capital, we are labourers, we are not in charge of the national debt.

Nicholas Jay Boyes
Milwaukee Wisconsin
American Democratic Republic
4 9 2014 11:38 P.M. Central Time (US)

On Crimean Russia and Ecology

Just what exactly Russia was thinking when they annexed Crimea recently is not clear. Crimea looks like an island in a warm climate, on the Black Sea. Compared to rough Russian winters it looks like a nice tropical alternative.

Unfortunately there is something it lacks: its water supply is 80% dependent on a single canal from the Dnieper, which flows south on to the isthmus through Ukraine.

This is a problem that will soon result in the loss of most of the crops grown in the Crimea, as the revolution in Ukraine has cut off the water to this canal.

Crimea will shortly revert to what it probably always was, basically a desert island. The rivers dried, the trees not replanted, all pointing to ecological failure in short order.

Again we must ask: why would Putin risk war to secure this small deserted region?

See also: http://www.bbc.com/news/world-europe-27155885

It makes you realize how precious water is. For a Great Lakes people, we must never allow 20th century pollution to return to our waters. Nuclear power must cease; its spent nuclear waste is still kept in Lake Michigan's water, to cool it. It must be removed to a safer location. It is an accident waiting to happen, in Point Beach and Waukegan. Recycling reduces the energy required to produce commodities. The Great lakes regions energy comes from primarily coal and nuclear. Coal is a local product, from Illinois and Kentucky. Unfortunately it is a fossil fuel, and subsequently causes global warming. It's burning also causes SO2 and NO2 emissions, which acidify the lake, Acid rain. This releases the naturally occurring Mercury in the rocks, resulting in fish unable to be eaten.

Renewable energy such as biomass, a good wood stove, could help out with the cold winter. Wood is a fun way to heat the house, and is cheaper than natural gas, coal, or nuclear. Theoretically it is renewable, if you replant good trees they will grow and one day replace the non-pristine forest already disturbed. In other words if you do find pristine forest leave it alone. Anything that is not going to come back must be left alone.

Crimea is looking like a costly failure. Trading for gas for Ukraine may be a short-term solution for the Crimea. The Coup leaders are merciless; they will reduce the Crimea to a desert by cutting off the water. They are not environmentalists, and should not be mistaken as. Until Crimea is reforested the rivers will remain dry. But without water to start with, as trees need love and water from a human being with a hose in that environment, the farms will fail and Crimea will be an unprofitable adventure for capitalists like Putin.

Nicholas Jay Boyes
Milwaukee Wisconsin
American Democratic Republic
4 28 2014 10:59 P.M. Central Time (US)

Conditions in Ukraine

It was a Sunday when the sanction of Universal Suffrage was given to the new leader of Ukraine. The East of Ukraine was still too lawless, but nevertheless the majority of Ukrainians voted in a new leader, Petro Poroshenko.

Mr. Poroshenko, a billionaire, gave a new face to Ukraine, whose past leaders were also mostly members of the Orange revolution too that removed the workers from control of the means of production, and expropriated their assets to billionaires like Poroshenko.

There has been turmoil in the country for years, and the recent overthrow of Yanukovich in a Coup De Tet, where the last elected leader was violently removed by the bourgeoisie.

Thus the replacement of Coup De Tet by a more bourgeois movement was completed today.

Russia was no longer able to control their borders, as they used to be under the Soviet Union.

The Western bourgeoisie finally had a victory over the remnants of the workers experiment with Marxism of Vladimir Lenin.
Undoubtedly the Iron bells tolled, the Maidan Movement victorious over the voices of the Union Man. The Maidan billionaires were officially accepted by western capitalists, with a bourgeois leader.

A truly historical day.

Nicholas Jay Boyes
Milwaukee Wisconsin
American Democratic Republic
5 25 2014 7:37 P.M. Central Time (US)

Letter to Russian Communist Party on Ukraine

Comrades

It is not clear to me exactly what Gazprom, the nationalized oil, represents. On one hand, I am glad it is not yet property of the bourgeoisie, as it is not creating surplus value.

In this respect like it. Nationalized industry is effective, and Gazprom is able to trade petroleum at market prices competitive on the world market.

Of course, the bourgeoisie also likes the state sometimes. National Debt, providing the capitalist with a place to put money otherwise unproductively invested, by giving an interest rate on the moneys held, which can only be called a form of capital.

The University system and the number of market occupations, all paid for with state money...

Obviously the taxman is a member of the bourgeoisie, although he is subordinate to capitalists.

So Gazprom is not clear to me. If it is running a surplus, it will be used as rent or surplus value for the capitalists as it will be expropriated in short order.

Now we meet Ukraine, where the Gas Queen Yulia still has a following although her life was spent expropriating workers property in petroleum.

The Coup De Tet recently, which only strengthened the bourgeoisie in Ukraine, resulting in a billionaire Poroshenko taking power, who only was able to have a limited sort of democracy, after the Communists were violently removed from parliament in the dictatorship which followed the Coup, sort of a farce of Universal Suffrage.

This much is clear to me about Gazprom: the Russian government, who is in control of the nationalized industry, has a right to trade with anyone they please, short of fascists. And the latter are a persistent aspect of East Europe, our proud pasts as royalist blood, Knights, nobles, etc.

If Russians do not want to trade oil with the Coup De Tet government in Ukraine, it is no ones business but Russia. Even if Ukrainian's bourgeoisie have the money to pay for the product, it is a matter of choice not of the west, but of Russia to trade.

Trade disputes erupt often with capitalists, like in Milwaukee where half the city was built by two different capitalists, Juneau and Kilbourne. They were so at odds the grid does not fit together over the Milwaukee River, resulting in engineering challenges a hundred years later.

The point is if Russia tells Ukraine to get oil elsewhere, and cuts off the flow through the territory due to dishonest businessman, it is their right to do this.

The Ukrainians have no one to thank for their debts they are currently owing to Russia but themselves. They made their beds now they can sleep in them. Gazprom has no legal obligation to provide any petroleum to any customers regardless of if they can pay, but especially when they cannot pay past debts to Gazprom for delivery of petroleum already used.

Nicholas Jay Boyes
Milwaukee Wisconsin
American Democratic Republic
6 9 2014 3:52 P.M. Central Time (US)

Letter to Russian Communist Party on Jews and Putin

Comrades

Of late the Prime Minister has met with the Jewish Chasids. This seems to have been the first thing he did after visiting Cuba.

Cuba should be a window into the world of the Americans. Only 90 miles away from the coast (150Km.) Cuba is close enough to America to really see the way the economic and political system is functioning.

As of late, the struggle between capital and labour continues. But we have some new friends, who have also experienced the types of oppression we have faced due to our feelings toward labour unions and surplus value.

They have been here all along and are treated the same as us, often oppressed by the Christian bourgeoisie, just like Marxists.

The Chasids have a few years on us; our communist movement is only a few hundred years old, whereas Israel is ancient.

Humanists, those of us who feel Christianity was a step backwards for humanity, may find in the Jews ancient culture and religion still intact from the Greek and Roman times, prior to Rome's fall.

Agora, the film, is an excellent account of the fall of the Great library of Alexandria to Christians. The barbaric flaying of Apacia the librarian by her own slave, the depths of the real thing of what happens if you let Christians take power.

Similar occurrences such as destruction of the temple of Apollo and the end of the temple of Delphi, the oracle, mark the barbarity of this movement.

Just what exactly do the Hasidic think of this group who assesses them as heathen, the same threat as the ancients?

Given their language is now Hebrew, an ancient language, anti Semitism would place them as the heathen, the communists of old.

The fact Putin reached out to them, even with the obvious blight of the war in Israel, is good. If nothing else it shows the legality of the culture, although to many the connection nominally between opposition to anti Semitism, and promoting socialism remains invisible.

We should welcome the Jewish workers as friends, in a struggle old and long from decided. We share common goals, atheists have a right to too not follow Christianity. I think the Chasids recognize this and have respect. And perhaps there are some of us who think the world was better off without Christians. This is an alternative, and if one decides this is his path, it is his life. I prefer a relationship of respect for Jews, although differences in philosophy and probably economics are present.

Nicholas Jay Boyes
Milwaukee Wisconsin
American Democratic Republic
7 13 2014 4:41 P.M. Central Time (US)

On the Civil War in Iraq

It was 1991 and the United States and the United Nations had invaded Iraq for the first time. They said the invasion of Kuwait, which forced the Crown Prince Al Sabah to abdicate his throne, was illegal. Consequently Iraq became the target of hatred from all the Muslim world who were royalist, for example from the Saudi Arabians, a kingdom whose leadership were all descended from the House of Suad, bred in Harams. The sons of the king run the country to this day. They are Sunni Muslims, and have Mecca, a place of religious significance to the followers of Mohammed.

Saddam Hussein would be forced by America to return to Iraq, and the Crown Prince Al Sabah was allowed to continue his dictatorial rule, to date 2014 he is still in power...

In 2003, March 20, America again attacked Iraq. This time it was fear of non-conventional weapons held by Saddam Hussein, who had survived the first attack on Iraq as leader.

This time it was not George 1 but George 2. It looked like Hussein could not rid himself of the Bushes; they continued to harass and intimidate Hussein until he was finally caught hiding in a trench in 2003. He was executed by the American created occupation government 3 years later.

But the conflict was yet to be solved. There was still the question of the nuclear weapons. Tony Blair, Prime Minister of Britain so famously went on television telling his population Iraq could attack England in 45 minutes with a nuclear weapon.

This of course proved to be as ridiculous as his constant claims of a fictitious "UN Mandate" to be in Iraq (the United Nations claimed the war in Iraq was illegal, noting no such non conventional weapons of any sort were found).

Undeterred the Americans continued bombing Iraq. It lasted until Barak Obama, who winning the contest of Universal Suffrage became

America's first black president, ran his election on his desire to remove the soldiers from Iraq.

The elections were a real show of just how the American worker felt abort having their sons put in a war overseas with little or no rational justification but plunder and occupation for the sake of oil profits, which was still a gamble.

Barak Obama looked like he had respected the wishes of the American people, and America was out of Iraq by the 18th of December 2011. So things were done?

In the summer of 2014 the Iraqis were close to a complete rout of the American installed government, they had half of Iraq, and were closing in at date of writing on Baghdad.

What did our anti war president do? He sent in 600 armed soldiers, a third invasion, armed to the teeth with drone aircraft, night vision goggles, etc.

It is frightening to think another war is now raging. Obama many times said he wanted no boots on the ground in Iraq of late.

But there go the young men again overseas, who fight for capitalism as we know it.

How could Barak Obama give up his main election pledge, to end the war in Iraq?

The American Democratic Republic has many faces, most shrouded in secrecy. Barak Obama is a public one, and does really have the power to command the army. But how many times have we heard the election promises derail? Scott Walker destroyed many labour unions all the time attempting to convince the Wisconsin workers he was creating jobs. He promised 250,000 new jobs in Wisconsin, and couldn't even create a quarter of this number as of late, and he is up for reelection in about 3 months...

On the Civil War in Iraq

The proletariat is not so easily taken. Obama's failed promises will demoralize the men who supported him. The elections may or may not turn against Obama, lets face it the Party of Obama is hell bent on having wife of fascist leader Bill Clinton as the face of the party after Obama steps down. And the "Republican" party is dominated by the reactionary bourgeoisie, totally reliant upon German scientists and other rejects who escaped the workers in Eastern Europe when the wall fell in 91'. They are atrocious, and are a reaction most Americans, unfamiliar with real anti Semitism, would never support if they knew the truth about these reactionaries. So expect the election to be decided by half or less of the registered voters, a public poll to see just where folks are standing, and a determined bourgeoisie with lots of cash to spend to receive the sanction of Universal Suffrage.

Nicholas Jay Boyes
Milwaukee Wisconsin
American Democratic Republic
6 30 2014 7:15 P.M. Central Time (US)

A Little Philosophy off the Front in Milwaukee

In my years of writing, in particular with the Internet, I have been in contact with many parties. Generally I find they are toothless, and when it seems like your making progress everything just falls through. It would seem to be that most people in the world and their parties, ad nauseum the capitalist ones, are only considering the brief period of time their party is elected, or their own personal empire.

"Everything has changed except our ideas." Albert Einstein

And no one is ever going to come and save you.

Generally it is only the bourgeoisie who can get elected, become fluent enough in a foreign language to make a difference there, have the money necessary to travel there and actually make friends.
Armed to the teeth against capitalists, with one chance in a generation to release us from the bondage of capitalism, the Soviet Union left us in the dark and went back to Putin, Yeltsin and unbridled free market capitalism.

America will not be bringing socialism to Russia anytime soon.

Russia will not be bringing socialism to America anytime soon.

You had best get over any illusions about someone coming and freeing you from the bondage of production for surplus value anytime soon. No one said the world would fix itself. It requires vision, and the ability to carry heavy burdens. Things can get better, it doesn't have to be like this. But it is a statement of weakness generally when a people asks a foreign military power to free them, Poland, with Katyn, Ukraine, with the decades bourgeoisie in America, Georgia and NATO, Syrian rebels and America etc.

If you free your body from the chains, the minds will follow. It is not the other way around.

Nicholas Jay Boyes
American Democratic Republic
8 25 2014 11:10 P.M. Central Time (US)

On the Civil War in Iraq

America's involvement in Iraq continued today with Barack Obama authorizing more bombings, and according to the New York Times:

http://www.nytimes.com/2014/08/08/world/middleeast/obama-weighs-military-strikes-to-aid-trapped-iraqis-officials-say.html

Kurdish and northern Iraqis say the bombing has already begun. Surgical Bombing, Defensive Air Power, Air Strikes etc. all involve civilians. Will it be on our screen every night, children pulled from rubble, hospitals overflowing, like the recent war in Israel? Will the world all watch as Iraq's children are shown the brutality of war? Was America attacked? At least Israel can point to a barrage of missiles striking the heart of their country…

No. It will not make American news. No crying children etc. Just a whitewashed story of the glory of the bourgeoisie, complete with German technology to better cover up the real cost of war.
Israel's latest war was uncomfortable to all of us. Iraq should be just as much so. Bill Clinton bombed Iraq, after the first invasion by George I. They called it the "no fly zone" that time and the rubble kept on rumbling. Of course, George II had to outdo George I, but Obama won the sanction of Universal Suffrage, full of promises to end the war. Well it definitely is not occurring today. Often in American politics there are timelines, dates promised when things will occur. Crossing these times is something even reactionary bourgeois have problems with. Congress creates bills for a certain time, like a financial bill for government funding. The bourgeoisie finds the money from the taxman, who gets it through the system of profit, essentially from the selling of commodities, based on the exploitation of wage labour. But the important part is the money is found, and it is for a certain time period, and given a certain date.

Apparently war is different. Now it seems the Treasury is wide open to Obama to use its money for the war overseas, with no Congressional backlash.

Israel again. How many Anti Semitist demonstrations occurred because of the news coverage of the horrors of what we today know as regular war? The Islamic world knows war. Mohammed was a military leader who invaded Mecca and made it holy for Muslims. This group was descended from Christians, who also used war upon gaining power in Rome to remove the ancient Greeks and Romans. They also removed the Jewish people when Rome fell to the German Odacer in the 5th century. Or are we to believe they were spared? The library of Alexandria was destroyed in Egypt; the Christians were there, they came through Israel to get there.

Warfare and religion seem to always be connected in the Western world. The bourgeoisie is still warring in Iraq, and now the atrocity of having to hide it from the workers in America whose children are being asked to fight in a war overseas they know little about. Obama's statements remind me of Putin's lies about involvement in Ukraine, after he annexed Crimea, yet now denies Russia is in Ukraine. The one armed bandit has returned to Crimea, Ukraine is now under a Billionaire, just now coming out of dictatorship from a Coup De Tet. Ukraine, another friend of America's bourgeoisie, looking more like just the way war is waged today, no boundaries, religious, moral, ethical etc..

The wars are all about control of markets. They are not workers striking in factories, leading the people to remove the surplus value creating mechanism, where workers are not paid for a portion of their workday, rather it is the property of the owner class. The wars are for the control of oil, and other commodities capitalistically produced upon expropriation from the labourers especially in Eastern Europe, but also in Iraq where the oil was once the nationally owned Iraq National Oil under Saddam Hussein. Obama seems to have expropriated the oil for Exxon Mobil, the most profitable company on Earth.

The war has not yet ended in Iraq. Obama's election commercial advertisements were all talk. America has no intention of letting all that oil just go the Iraqis. It may be some time before we see an end to this conflict....

On the Civil War in Iraq

Nicholas Jay Boyes
Milwaukee Wisconsin
American Democratic Republic
8 7 2014 10:19 P.M. Central Time (US)

Letter to Russian Communist Party

Comrades

As violence continues to flare in Ukraine, it looks like Eastern Europe is starting to have Coup de Tet's again. Now on Russia's doorstep to the west we see chaos and bloodshed as the reactionary bourgeoisie Poroshenko fights the liberal progressive bourgeoisie of Putin.

It would seem to be the right time to ask: should Russia follow suite of Ukraine?

Could Russia have dictatorship of the proletariat a year or so, then have elections without the reactionary bourgeoisie?

Clearly the Communist Party can no longer feel secure from violence in Ukraine; they were removed from parliament for speaking with their other freely elected officials. No one needs to feel guilty if the party refuses to take part in the parliament; I know I would not be up for a bloody nose if I gave a speech.

It has generally been like Russia to fight back against the fascists by doing what they do right back to them, to build the industry used by the bourgeoisie, to not fall behind. To respond to provocations with countermeasures, not disproportionate, but appropriate for the moment.

NATO condones Coup De Tet in Ukraine. Perhaps Russia could have a revolution, resembling other Eastern European powers like Ukraine now that this is legal, and not worry about Universal Suffrage until the Communist Party is in power, then have elections that would be as fair as NATO sanctioned Universal Suffrage in Ukraine.

Nicholas Jay Boyes
Milwaukee Wisconsin
American Democratic Republic
8 15 2014 11:05 P.M. Central Time (US)

On the Workers Movement by Nicholas Jay Boyes

There is a saying in capitalist America by the men who own the financial capital, and the means of production:

"Time is money.

This is true. The more hours the labourer can be made to work, the maximum until he gets to worn out or otherwise gets ill to continue labouring, the more surplus value, the unpaid hours of labour.
An increase of relative surplus value is always promised by the political structure of the bourgeoisie, especially during the contests of Universal Suffrage. The worker is supposed to be happy with this, what is happening is the machinery is getting more advanced, and the hours labored relative to the amount of product decreases. The capitalist gets rewarded by selling the increased volume of commodities, but it is the labour in the material product he is really selling.

If the wages of labour remain constant, the capitalist makes more surplus value by having a more commodities to sell; he has paid less for the same amount of labour by advancing the machinery, the constant capital. The increase is pocketed by the capitalist, resulting in more relative surplus value being created. It is relative to the labourers wages.

If wages rise, or new jobs are created (an increased variable capital expenditure) it is possible the increase of relative surplus value will create a profit that will benefit the worker. In fact this is the object of the Liberal bourgeoisie, But it overlooks the fact the labourer is not laboring voluntarily; he is not freely selling his labour. The other capitalists would pay less for the same commodity somewhere else, where wages were lower and profits higher.

What can the worker really be promised if there is some form of revolution? What will society be like if the surplus value driven production is finally brought to a unceremonious end?

Time is money.

The worker will have more time off work, as he will no longer work without pay for a large segment of the workday.

The revolution may not bring large amounts of gold, faster sports autos, yachts for pleasure, etc.

But the worker will have time and a basic standard of living in line with what he has been currently receiving as wages from the now defunct capitalist for less hours laboured.

The time left free can be used by the labourer to create art, study philosophy, or any other endeavor. An 8 hour day is the start of this Union movement, and without a capitalist it could be lowered further as we have more advanced machinery than the 19th century when we first came up with this goal.

So to the folks who cannot live without their bourgeois needs, life may not be the same. But for the majority of society who work for a living, who receive wages from the capitalist to make their bread, life will improve. This is the essence of communism, brought to our attention by Karl Marx.

Nicholas Jay Boyes
Milwaukee Wisconsin
American Democratic Republic
8 29 2014 1:41 P.M. Central Time (US)

On the Continuing War in Iraq

It would seem that, in his televised speech just a few hours ago today, one day before the 13th anniversary of 9 11, the day we remember the attack in New York, Obama, like George Bush, again chose war as an option in Iraq, regardless of the fact Iraq had nothing to do with 9 11. The original attack was carried out by Osama Bin Laden, and contrary to popular opinion, inside plantings of bombs occurred in American structures in New York.

Nevertheless there is no reason to believe Osama Bin Laden was not connected to, or coordinated as leader the attacks...

Barack Obama caught Bin Laden, and executed him. How was it done? With a fake vaccination project in Pakistan. They found Bin Laden's DNA and killed him.

Pretty crafty but a few things strike as strange this story, Pakistan, not Afghanistan is where Bin Laden was hiding. Why was not Afghanistan, where the 13 year war still rages today, where the leader supposedly was hiding? Could he have led Al Qaeda from a foreign country?

With all due respects to America's public health programs, vaccination is sort of more a Red Cross mission. Will disease be eliminated when people are fearing vaccinations?

So Obama seems to have decided to bomb Iraq again. The German technology, jet aircraft, rockets, etc. was all gained from the German scientists of the 20th century, who through Project Paperclip were sanctioned to work in the United States, even though they took part in Nazi atrocities as scientists and doctors, created German like material conditions in America.

The same industry that has only brought us war, especially the V2 rockets, now used again in Iraq by the bourgeoisie.

Jet aircraft may get us across the ocean faster, a side effect of military research to conquer the Soviet Union. But it is no substitute for the passenger train for land travel.

The petroleum sports cars on the Autobahn, another Hitler industry, also have made America dependent of fossil fuels to satisfy its transportation problems. Hitler invented Superhighways, later designed in America after the war, probably with the help of German engineering. What is required to operate this system? What just happens to be under Iraq in massive quantities, petroleum.

The petroleum in Iraq prior to the first war there was nationalized as the Iraqi National Oil Company. Saddam Hussein may have been a tyrant but he did keep the oil for the good of the Iraq people after he built his palaces, the likes of which compared to the wealth that is now destined for Exxon Mobile look like poverty.

Obama told us he was not going to fight war in Iraq; it was something he promised us twice to vote for him. It was effective, as the workers in America have overwhelmingly rejected war in Iraq, to the point it is rare even to see the opposition reactionary bourgeoisie, the "Republicans" come out in favor of the violence there. Given their own responsibility for the latest war there, created by the second Bush, reactionary, I guess seals their fate as warriors there.

But Obama descended from the liberal progressive bourgeoisie of late we have been voting for as an alternative to the reliance on German technology, with the reactionary bourgeoisie supporters of more petroleum industry, designed by the 20th century Germans.
Just how far up in the air does one have to be to not be in some else's space? Outer Space?

The Jet Aircraft are in someone else's space and are we to believe there are no Americans on the ground, even to just confirm a successful bombing? Do they really trust the Iraqi army that much, to let them determine what victory is?

On the Continuing War in Iraq

Unless you were born yesterday, you must see the war is still raging, although it stopped briefly. And now it is Obama, our peace candidate, sanctioning violence overseas. It looks like America is headed towards another endless commitment to war, until they are conquered, just like Vietnam.

Nicholas Jay Boyes
Milwaukee Wisconsin
American Democratic Republic
9 10 10:06 P.M. Central Time (US)

On the Scottish Referendum

With the results of the Scottish referendum now in, 45% to 55%, clearly the United Kingdom remains, a victory for the bourgeoisie.

"With the results in from all 32 council areas, the "No" side won with 2,001,926 votes over 1,617,989 for "Yes". "

BBC News Scotland September 19, 2014

Even Obama supported the Queen in the end, much like Uncle Tom from Uncle Tom's cabin, who gets the money for the slave owner from the free north only to get sold down the river by the Southern plantation owner.

There was a time in the 19th century the British sailors who were against the queen used to mutiny the boats to America's shores.

How tame Obama and the Americans have become.

The only real question now is what went wrong? There were many failures:

1. Failure to clearly show the Queen would be abdicating the throne if the Yes side won
2. The anti Semitism and Israel
3. Whether or not to join the European Union
4. Assuming the nuclear weapons had to go were the nuclear power electrical production facilities to stay
5. Inability to link town and country

These 5 points should have been openly addressed. Without a clear picture of these points it is remarkable the yes side received 45% of the vote.

I have no doubt that had the vote been to remove the queen it would have looked different. It seems every night the royals are on American Television screens, ad naseum. If the Scots are sick of it they should have come out with it and overthrown the monarchy in a democratic vote and been done with her. Instead it was not clear if she was staying as the head of state.

That is how you lose.

The question of the anti Semitism and the parties feelings towards Israel was wrong. There was no Hasidic representation in the Yes camp. Where were Scotland's Jews? Instead it was the plight of the Palestinians, whose religion does not allow them to assimilate Jewish culture and live in Israel. Instead they have been trying to destroy Israel for years. It is not clear to me why all socialists should not support Israel. The Palestinians are far more committed to religion and royalist governments as Muslims, and the war with the Muslims in the region continues. The Israelis nominally should have been the clear choice of the Scots.

As far as joining the European Union, it is aligned with Germany and NATO. If they were anti nuclear they should have rejected NATO and shut down the nuclear electrical production facilities while moving out the nuclear submarines and nuclear bombs of the bourgeoisie, regardless of the threat of the anthropocentric yet still revolutionary working class communist movements.

The gap between town and country was clearly visible in the vote. The proletariat in Glasgow supported the referendum, yet his cousins in the countryside were unable to grasp the message, for the reasons I have stated. With agriculture so machinery oriented, there is not much difference between the farmer and the proletariat. Yet the divisions, lack of communication and without strong leadership of Glasgow's revolutionaries, due to capitalism town and country was kept divided. These are a few of the reasons the independence vote failed. It is not clear if it will happen again in my lifetime. If it does I will be happy, but this type of thing is rare.

Nicholas Jay Boyes
Milwaukee Wisconsin

On the Scottish Referendum

American Democratic Republic
9 19 2014 11:09 A.M. Central Time (US)

On Current Historical Material Conditions and Political Organization

The current view of Great Britain after the failed referendum by Scotland to secede must be shifting. Previously they looked like a vibrant democracy, albeit absent a real Communist Party opposition but a Labour party that could at least nominally claim to be an alternative to unbridled capitalism German style.

Now we see all parties were united in keeping the United Kingdom precisely what it is and remains, a kingdom. The crotchets of the 20th century bourgeoisie were fully present in the event. Every time the British looked like they were losing they started issuing threats of moving capital out, a failed currency, etc. on the BBC. In victory concessions were always promised, concessions that have yet to materialize for Scotland.

A small dictatorship, under the Queen and House of Lords with a tame opposition of free market capitalists in Parliament under a bourgeoisie of David Cameron, a well bred Englishman representative of the upper classes of the island, is what we saw claim victory.

A House of Lords, the upper house of parliament, appointed with the blessing of the Queen, a dictatorship with hereditary titles to land ownership, whose only real tie to any small forms of universal suffrage are they are given the approval of parliament prior to their installment by the Queen, and do not include her removal as the head of state as a goal.

A United Party structure all against independence for Scotland. All Parties, Labour, Liberal Democrats and the ruling Conservative Party all in favor of keeping the Queen in Scotland permanently. The value of democracy, Universal Suffrage, is the question of the decade. It has been burning for some time, with the fall of the Soviet Union and a limited democracy. But what exactly is democracy when the nominal head of state is a dictator who inherits power to her children and rules with no end except her death? And this is considered civilized in the place where one is led to believe industrial conditions are most advanced, where people are enjoying a fine standard of living, and seem not to be violently attempting to overthrow their government in strike after strike by disgruntled labourers constantly.

And she is not alone. Spain, Belgium, The Netherlands, Sweden, Norway among other smaller Western European states all have a feudal head of state who is not elected.

It is not some form of socialism. The Queen is the epitome of inheritance. Her wealth and power is transferred to her children by right of birth. She is not there by the grace of the united working class of the Communist Party.

How anyone could possibly call this bourgeoisie anything other than dictatorship is like thinking the taxman is a member of the socialist party, some sort of Robin Hood who can tax the rich.

So today we see Hong Kong experiencing revolutionary upheaval, calling themselves the Occupy after the groups in America attempting to have a socialist revolution, who tried to shut down the New York Stock Exchange. Given Britain's rule by the Queen (which was the most recent form of democracy they experienced) and the forms of political activity under this dictator why do these people feel they should be included in America's militant proletariat? It looks like National Socialism.

We must remember these Western European societies have many fervent supporters in their countries and outside who believe they experience democracy, yet are under royal heads of state. Will the Hong Kong residents appeal to the Europeans, the same bourgeoisie they did not have a democracy under, they were ruled by Queen Elizabeth as a colony, for Universal Suffrage? Will our President like Uncle Tom support the feudal royalty, the same royalty who transported and enslaved most of the Africans in America to begin with?

Letter to Greenpeace

I don't know exactly what democracy is. I don't know if anybody does. As a proletariat all I know is I have no country. Nevertheless one man one vote regardless of race or class is a powerful argument, one that seems to be one a man must fight for to achieve rather than simply inherit like a royal title.

Nicholas Jay Boyes
Milwaukee Wisconsin
American Democratic Republic
10 4 2014 3:09 P.M. Central Time (US)

Letter to Greenpeace

Friends

The pursuit of nuclear energy for electrical generation is a product of the consciousness of the 20th century, an anthropocentric idea of any means necessary to provide for the human being, at the expense of the ecology.

Even the communism experienced in the 20th century, the Soviet Union, an advanced experiment of the working class, still failed to recognize what would be the shift in consciousness of the ecological human being vs. the anthropocentric, a shift in the new millennium.

The strange part is Karl Marx, the most advanced of the socialist thinkers, was alive to read Darwin, who in many ways was a forerunner of the ecological movement that would begin to take place in the end of the 20th century. Marx had read the Descent of Man, and agreed with the conclusions. Marx believed in Darwin as he was a materialist, and agreed man created himself through evolution, as opposed to creation by Jesus Christ, which puts mans development as an external phenomenon created the latter, 7 days of creation, Adam and Eve, etc.

Capitalism 20th century style resulted in Fascism. The material conditions that led to this ideology were V2 Rockets, Autobahns, fossil fuels...

Nuclear energy was largely the product of Eisenhower's Atoms for Peace project, which shared nuclear reactors with many less materially developed cultures, resulting in the spread of nuclear weapons and pollution we know today as the remnants of the nuclear industry.

It is still being practiced by capitalism:

"It's simply impossible to find sufficient financial backing unless countries are willing to sell themselves out completely to Russia's Rosatom and

Vladimir Putin's financial and energy moguls, as Hungary and Finland are currently doing.

Greenpeace article dated 10 9 2014

http://www.greenpeace.org/international/en/news/Blogs/nuclear-reaction/the-european-commissions-nuclear-decision-thr/blog/50928/

Russia reverted to capitalism in 1989, after all of its satellite states also reverted to capitalism in the same period of the late 20th century. It should be of no surprise a return to fascism resulted, secretly and openly, especially Estonia, Georgia, and Ukraine.

In the failure of the Soviets, another factor leading to the failure of this anthropocentric vision of Russian socialism was the meltdown of the Chernobyl reactor. Unfortunately the Coup De Tet government in Ukraine was not anti nuclear, and remains in favor of nuclear energy. The people did not take to the streets in peaceful anti nuclear demonstrations.

Nevertheless this use of fission is still popular in Russia. And they are expanding it outside their borders. It is no longer revolutionary, if it ever was. It is outdated, and should be left in the past after the Chernobyl incident, and Fukashima Diachi as of late.

Russia is motivated by competition, which has returned as a value of the economic system of capitalism. In this respect it is far harder to rationalize with the Putin led government. The Communist Party there is far more understanding of the rights of the labourer, and having to live downwind from a factory producing fission a real curse I think they fully understand.

The nuclear industry is no longer in the hands of the socialists, nevertheless it is unfortunate they lacked vision to not produce this type of industry to begin with. Live and learn. I would be surprised to see nuclear energy a serious competitor to recycling and Renewable energy in the new millennium. The purpose of industry now is to reduce mans negative impact on the environment. And this shift even capitalism will never be able to stop…

Letter to Greenpeace

Nicholas Jay Boyes
Milwaukee Wisconsin
American Democratic Republic
10 9 2014 10:20 P.M. Central Time(US)

On a Free Press

There is a movement to keep a close watch on those who disagree with the capitalist system in America. They call it surveillance, and it is a military activity.

There are many high tech ways to accomplish this, and it gets bloody and ugly the more you learn about it.

Simply being watched by a telephone or television with a radio in it is nothing. Surveillance can be far more invasive…

The real problem is once the offending message or expression of feelings of the party being surveilled, what to do about this expression?

The next step is censorship.

Surveillance is a step toward censorship. Isolate and identify the offending parties, and attempt to make the message disappear, often violently.

This is the inherent danger in the police state revealed to us by the defectors like Edward Snowden.

Freedom of expression is a battle to maintain. In a capitalist state like America the struggle never ends. It seems like every day we hear the bourgeoisie asking for more surveillance, and the weapons to do so.

A censored press has been more difficult to maintain with the Internet. But where has this industry come from? The same military structure capitalists created to control the activities of the human being.

The protests, the strikes, all drive toward lifting the surveillance state, and respect freedom of expression. Karl Marx began his career writing against the Prussian censorship laws. It is a revolutionary goal you work for your entire life.

Freedom of expression is not compatible with surveillance.

Surveillance is one more step towards censorship.

Nicholas Jay Boyes
Milwaukee Wisconsin
American Democratic Republic
11 30 2014 9:47 P.M. Central Time

www.ingramcontent.com/pod-product-compliance
Lightning Source LLC
Chambersburg PA
CBHW022018170526
45157CB00003B/1271